# GOVERNING SECURITY

'This challenging book by two of the world's leading authorities on policing and private security is a landmark in scholarship and debate on the subject. It argues for a reconceptualisation of the fields of policing and crime control in terms of a broader, comprehensive notion of the governance of security. It is the most wide-ranging and persuasive interpretation to date of contemporary changes in policing. Thought-provoking and informative, it will attract much debate and remain a fundamental reference point for a long time to come.'

*Professor Robert Reiner, London School of Economics*

Governance has been radically transformed over the past several decades. These transformations have been mirrored in, and often prefigured by, changes in the governance of security – the mentalities, institutions, technologies and practices used to promote secure environments. This book traces the nature of these governmental changes by looking at security. It examines a variety of related questions, including:

- What significant changes have occurred in the governance of security?
- What implications do these changes have for collective life?
- What new imaginings may be needed to reshape security?
- What ethical factors need to be considered in formulating such new imaginings?

The authors conclude by bringing together descriptive, explanatory and normative considerations to assess how justice can be conceived within the governance of security. This book will be of interest to students and academics working in the fields of governance and politics, criminology and policing, and justice and security studies.

**Les Johnston** is a professor of criminology and Research Director at the Institute of Criminal Justice Studies, University of Portsmouth.

**Clifford Shearing** is a professor in the Law Program, Research School of Social Sciences, Australian National University and in the School of Government at the University of the Western Cape.

# GOVERNING SECURITY

## Explorations in policing and justice

*Les Johnston and Clifford Shearing*

Routledge
Taylor & Francis Group

LONDON AND NEW YORK

First published 2003
by Routledge
11 New Fetter Lane, London EC4P 4EE

Simultaneously published in the USA and Canada
by Routledge
29 West 35th Street, New York, NY 10001

*Routledge is an imprint of the Taylor & Francis Group*

Typeset in Sabon by
BOOK NOW Ltd
Printed and bound in Great Britain by
TJ International Ltd, Padstow, Cornwall

*British Library Cataloguing in Publication Data*
A catalogue record for this book is available from the British Library

*Library of Congress Cataloging in Publication Data*
Johnston, Les.
Governing security : explorations in policing and justice / Les Johnston and
Clifford Shearing.
p. cm.
Includes bibliographical references and index.
1. Crime prevention–Philosophy. 2. Law enforcement–Philosophy. 3. Security
systems. 4. Police. 5. Criminal justice, Administration of. I. Shearing,
Clifford D., 1942–
II. Title.
HV7431 .J643 2003
363.1′001–dc21                                    2002068190

ISBN 0-415-14961-4 (hbk)
ISBN 0-415-14962-2 (pbk)

To our families, friends and
colleagues for enriching and
nourishing our lives and work

# CONTENTS

# 1

# INTRODUCTION
## Thinking about security

### Introducing security

'Am I going to be safe?' 'Are those around me going to be safe?' 'Are the things I value going to be safe?' These are questions that we ask ourselves, implicitly or explicitly, hundreds of times a day. When we can answer them affirmatively we feel at peace and may move forward with a sense of security. This feeling of peace underlies the term 'security' whose derivation may be traced to Latin words meaning 'without care' or, in modern colloquial parlance, 'care-free'. Sometimes that feeling of peace arises because we or others have taken particular initiatives to enhance our safety: women may carry rape alarms when travelling at night; anxious parents may choose to have their offspring vaccinated against certain childhood diseases, or equip them with cell phones when they are out at night; car owners may have sophisticated anti-theft devices fitted to their new vehicles. Yet, none of these initiatives necessarily guarantees a feeling of safety on the part of the person undertaking it, since each may itself give rise to other risks. For example, the anxious parents may have had to balance the benefits of vaccination (safety from measles and mumps) with its potential costs (the slim chance that the child might be damaged by it).

Nowadays, the term 'security' is applied to many different facets of our existence. It is used to refer to our personal, physical safety, as well as to the safety of our belongings from damage or depredation, but it is also used with respect to our emotional, psychological and financial well-being. We refer to collective programmes designed to ensure such well-being as 'social security' or the 'social safety net', and measures to protect the integrity of the state and its institutions as 'national security'. Conflicts that break out in various parts of the world are often referred to as threats to 'international peace and security'.

Important as security is to us, however, our desire to achieve it has to be balanced against other things that we value, such as liberty, privacy and justice. For example, people often say that they will accept a degree of insecurity rather than turn their homes into 'armed fortresses' in order to ensure their safety. While they might believe that having someone watch over them all the time would enhance their security, most people would regard the resulting loss of privacy as too high a price to pay for achieving that end. Similarly, the various 'due process' requirements that have been built into our criminal justice systems over the centuries reflect the view that the values of justice and liberty are considered to be just as important to us as the value of security. Of course, it is by no means easy to reconcile these different values. Recent controversy surrounding attempts to prosecute General Pinochet for 'crimes against humanity' in Chile, together with the work of the Truth and Reconciliation Commission in post-Apartheid South Africa, indicate the difficulties which may be encountered in trying to balance demands for justice and security. That is not to say that the two are irreconcilable. Later in this book we consider the relationship between security and justice in more detail. We argue that while tensions may exist between the two, they are also mutually interdependent. This means that if authorities want to govern security more effectively they are obliged to pursue justice more diligently.

People rarely have complete control over their own security and, although most of us strive to achieve as much control as possible, not everyone has the same capacity or opportunity to do so. To complicate matters further, security is also affected by external contingencies. Thus, we may feel safe (or unsafe) not because we have implemented (or failed to implement) an action to enhance our security, but because things happen over which we have relatively little control. People may feel more secure after interest rate cuts, landslide election victories, royal weddings or great national sporting victories; and less secure after bouts of galloping inflation, 'hung parliaments', royal scandals or national sporting disasters. Other factors, may be more closely linked to their local and immediate experience. Thus, people's security may be affected by their integration or lack of integration into local neighbourhood groups or by their wider involvement in local civil institutions. Though our primary concern in this book is with deliberate (intended) actions undertaken by people in pursuit of security, it is also important to be aware of the wide range of contingencies that may affect their sense of security.

2

Our subjective 'sense of security' (our feeling of safety) is just as important to most of us as any objective measure of our 'actual security' (i.e. the risks that we actually face). However, if the discrepancy between the two grows too wide, we are liable to be warned either that we have a 'false sense of security' or that we are 'paranoid'. Thus, to be effective, security measures must address our subjective perceptions as well as more objectively identifiable threats to our safety. For most of us, when we feel safe it is because we have confidence in the steps we, or others, have taken to promote security. Or, to put it another way, we feel safe because things have been done to govern security. This governance might be quite informal and fleeting as, for example, when we take precautions while engaged in some routine activity. At the other extreme the governance of security might be the result of a complex programme of action that is sustained through space and time and which may involve large numbers of people, sophisticated bureaucratic procedures, complicated budgetary calculations and the deployment of costly resources as, for example, in arrangements established by law enforcement agencies to 'keep the peace'.

By way of illustration consider two rather different examples. The first of these shows how security may be the product of mundane, everyday practices. One of us was recently involved in a piece of research which looked at the transitions experienced by a group of young people (aged 16–25) living on 'Willowdene', a housing estate in the North East of England. Willowdene is a surprisingly complex locality. On the one hand, it experiences all of the objective indicators of an excluded place, including excep-tionally high levels of unemployment, sickness, and school truancy, as well as high rates of crime and disorder. On the other hand, the impact of economic deprivation and exclusion on young people was far from simple since the transitions which they made from teenage years to adulthood were, with the exception of those engaged in criminal careers, surprisingly 'complex, multiple, non-linear, often disorderly and sometimes unpredictable' (Johnston *et al.*, 2000: 31). Young people living in this multiply-deprived locality managed to 'get by', sometimes through participation in further education, sometimes through gainful (often spasmodic) employment, some-times through engagement with the 'informal economy', and, as often as not, through a shifting combination of different means. This diverse process of 'getting by' was linked to young people's participation in local networks. Such networks were one of the means by which they managed their daily lives, using them to obtain work, to participate in leisure and to manage personal and family safety. For example, in an area where burglary is commonplace, access to appropriate networks – and, more particularly, to the knowledge contained within them – is crucial. If residents want to avoid becoming victims of burglary, it helps to be acquainted with, or at least to know others who are acquainted with, potential burglars. That way it may be possible to persuade them not to victimise you or, if you are victimised, to improve your chances of recovering your stolen goods. Having access to local knowledge was, therefore, crucial for the negotiation of day-to-day problems relating to security in Willowdene. Access to these networks and to the knowledge contained within them was vital for identifying whom it was safe to associate with, where it was safe to go, and when it was safe to go there. It was also important for defining young people as locals and for differentiating them from outsiders. These local networks bore a complex relationship to the problem of exclusion. On the one hand, their very reason for existence indicated the estate's exclusion vis-à-vis the wider area. On the other hand, their utility in helping people 'get by' provided a critical means for residents' inclusion within the Willowdene locality. In the case of Willowdene, then, the governance of young people's security was built into the routine, day-to-day, workings of local networks, rather than the product of an explicit security programme.

Our second example illustrates a different point and concerns the recent experience of one of us who had two friends visiting him in South Africa, one from Canada, the other from Germany. Both commented on how secure they felt when in the company of people in whom they had confidence as guarantors of their safety. When guided by such persons they went about their business feeling as safe as they would at home. This feeling covered a variety of different circumstances, from visiting the up-market parts of Cape Town, to driving in rural areas, or visiting informal settlements. Being at peace, they were able to concentrate on what they were doing, socialise, enjoy the scenery and so on. By contrast, when they had to negotiate things themselves, even when the places they were in and the people they were meeting were 'objectively' no more dangerous, their sense of safety was different. They had little confidence in the state's capacity to guarantee their security and even less confidence in their own ability to organise their lives in ways that would ensure their safety. When confident of security guarantees, they were relaxed, paid little attention to reports of crime in newspapers and discounted the concerns of people they talked to at 'home' about their safety. When lacking such confidence, they felt unprotected and their sense of South Africa as a place changed dramatically. The newspaper reports of danger became much more salient as did the concerns of their friends and family. Of course, in both circumstances they were unharmed and 'objectively' secure. Yet peace for them was not simply the absence of objective risk. It required an assurance that the safety they were experiencing was something they could rely upon as they moved from situation to situation over time.

What this example illustrates, in addition to the importance of the mobilisation of local knowledge and capacity in the governance of security, is the future-focused character of programmes for guaranteeing security. Such programmes not only seek to provide guarantees of safety at the present moment, but also to project them into the future. Peace is more than the mere absence of present threat; it embodies the sense that one *will be* safe in the future. For that reason peace requires a guarantee in which one has confidence and upon which one can rely. Thomas Hobbes, the seventeenth-century thinker who provided much of the framework for conceiving contemporary governance, articulated this sense of future safety when he argued that peace was like the weather. The statement 'the weather is fine' is not merely a description of the present ('it is not raining now in New York') but also a confident prediction of the future ('it will not rain in New York for the rest of the day'). Thus, it may be said, security comprises the confident belief that peace in our environment is assured both now and for some reasonably foreseeable future.

So far we have said that our interest in security lies in intentional actions whose purpose is to provide guarantees of safety to subjects, both in the present and in the future. Two further points may be added. First, the realisation of security is subject to empirical contingencies and cannot be taken for granted. It is one thing to offer guarantees of security to subjects. It is another to assume that they will be realised in practice. Thus, it is always possible that security initiatives and programmes will fall short of giving people an effective assurance of peace. Whether security is achieved in particular circumstances is, therefore, a matter of empirical (experiential) judgement. Second, because security is subject to the nuances of experience, it should not be regarded as an 'either–or' phenomenon – something dependent upon the mere presence or absence of given material conditions. We feel at secure and at peace when we perceive the risk of threat to be below our comfort threshold. Our comfort thresholds are not only determined by the threats we perceive, but also by the confidence we have in the mechanisms that seek to guarantee our peace. If we have confidence in these mechanisms we are inclined to see incidents of disorder as just that: as incidents. When we lack confidence we view them as emblematic of an underlying disorder and of the absence of any effective mechanisms for addressing that disorder. It is this feature of security that is recognised when people talk of the importance of responding to the fear of crime in addition to simply responding to the presence of crime.

The experiential character of security raises two further issues that are crucial to its governance. First, since individual comfort thresholds are not identical, what might be a peaceful situation for one person may not be so for another. Yet, we should not conclude from this that comfort thresholds may not be correlated. Often, one of the features of the collectivities we describe as 'communities' is a shared comfort threshold that underpins a common experience of peace. Second, people's individual and collective feelings about security have to be considered alongside their feelings about other human values and priorities such as effectiveness, value for money, propriety, accountability, liberty, privacy, equality and justice. Recognition of this fact poses major dilemmas for the governance of security. One such dilemma concerns the appropriate balance that might be struck between the pursuit of security and the pursuit of other values such as liberty. Another concerns the compatibility of security with these other values. For example, is it possible to achieve the democratic governance of security while, simultaneously, ensuring its just distribution?

## Security programmes

By now, the reader may have noticed that in discussing security we have made only a tangential reference to crime and no reference at all to criminology, policing or the police. This might seem strange in view of our professional backgrounds, each of us being employed for much of our professional lives within university criminology institutions and having written extensively on policing matters. We shall say more about our decision to conceive security initiatives in terms of 'governance' (rather than in the more conventional terms of 'policing') in a moment. For now, let it merely be said that this decision arises, in part, from a disenchantment with approaches which limit our understanding of the governance of security to a narrow range of actions undertaken by a limited number of specialist (state) agencies. The limits of that view are apparent as soon as one considers some of the rudimentary properties of security programmes.

Programmes that seek to guarantee peace involve six critical elements. First, they require a view of what security entails – a *definition of order*. Order, in this sense, connotes a prescription of the 'way things need to be' (e.g. which activities and behaviours should be permitted, and which proscribed) in order to ensure a secure environment. This prescription may be formally laid down in a set of statements, for example, as legislation, or it may be no more than an implicitly shared sense of order that is used to determine what we feel mechanisms for governing security should seek to accomplish. The criminal law is perhaps the most easily identified of such prescriptions, although local customs may be just as influential as prescriptions of order. What is common to all such prescriptions, however, is that they are products of some kind of political negotiation, that they almost always reflect some interests more than others and that they are commonly sites of contestation of some kind.

The second element is some *authority*, or more likely authorities, that seek to promote security, that is, a guarantor or guarantors. States have been and continue to be guarantors of security, and this responsibility is commonly expressed in their constitutions. The Canadian constitution, for instance, states that the Federal Parliament is responsible for making laws for the 'peace, order and good government' of the country. There are, however, many others. These others may be no more than people we know, and rely upon, to protect us, such as family members, friends, colleagues and neighbours. They are just as frequently other forms of government, such as the non-state, 'private governments' described by Mcauley (1986), which seek to promote secure places in which people can do business. Today these non-state governments are often corporate entities that assume responsibility for governing the spaces in which people live, work and play. The residential spaces we call 'gated communities' provide one example. Increasingly, the various authorities that govern security co-ordinate their activities to form networks of governance. An example is the networks that are established when residents accept responsibility for governing their own security through programmes such as Neighbourhood Watch. Typically, these programmes are organised in ways that co-ordinate police and community resources at the local level.

The remaining elements are closely related to one another. The third of these comprises the methods that programmes for governing security rely upon. We will call these methods *technologies*. These technologies are correlated with a fourth element: ways of thinking (or *mentalities*) that establish how issues of peace are constructed and addressed. Mentalities make order and disorder thinkable. As such, they provide the framework within which technologies are developed and practised. Since the exercise of technologies requires an infrastructure for applying resources, technologies are also correlated with a fifth element, *institutions* – structures which provide a means of organising and relating people and things. Finally, the result of the combination of these different elements is the production of a determinate security *practice*.

A very common technology is the threat or application of punishment to persuade people who might be tempted to undermine security to act in an orderly fashion. This technology, together with the mentality and institutional arrangements correlated with it, forms the basis of what we have come to think of as the 'criminal justice system'. The criminal justice system is a set of institutions employed by the state to guarantee security – though, as we shall see, the state's responsibility for guaranteeing other values, such as liberty, privacy and justice, places constraints on the design of state security mechanisms. While the criminal justice system is the institutional complex we tend to associate with the governance of security, it is not the only mechanism that is used to serve this end. However, because we have tended to conflate this mechanism with the governance of security we are inclined not to notice alternative mechanisms. This is true even though we rely on them constantly to provide guarantees of peace both in their own right and within networks that may include state mechanisms. Consequently, although we employ these other institutions and technologies of security regularly they tend to remain at the edges of our awareness – used but unnoticed.

To recognise the presence of these other mechanisms for guaranteeing security, however, we only need to reflect on the basis on which we answer questions about the existence or absence of peace. If, for instance, we respond to the advertising slogan not to 'leave home without it', and set off on our travels armed with an American Express Card, we are recognising and acting upon the effectiveness of the global guarantees of financial security which American Express offers its card holders, both alone and in conjunction with the many network partnerships that American Express can and does mobilise.

As we go about our daily lives a whole network of resources provides for our security. This typically includes a variety of corporate auspices, many of which, however, are only available to those who are already well off and 'successful'. An interesting, contemporary illustration is provided by companies who plan and execute what has come to be called 'incentive travel'. These companies arrange exotic trips for business people and their families who have won incentive awards. The awards enable them to enjoy wonderful meals and excursions in exotic places that are not accessible to others. These travellers (corporate denizens) are thus able to enjoy safe and peaceful holidays in countries where, outside the benefit of corporate guarantees of security, life is experienced as far from safe and peaceful. They travel in a world of safety that extends across national boundaries and that links secure enclaves. This concept of extending the developed world with its safety and luxury into the 'undeveloped' world has been pioneered by organisations like Club Med. When travellers take holidays with Club Med in some part of the world where the climate is good and the geography appealing, the world they live in belongs to a new corporately governed set of linked terrains that together comprise a new global space. A 'third place' that is neither entirely 'public' nor entirely 'private' as these terms have come to be defined within the paradigm of national sovereignty.

## Why the 'governance of security'?

In this book when we talk of the governance of security we will be referring, in particular, to programmes for promoting peace in the face of threats (either realised or anticipated) that arise from collective life rather than from non-human sources such as the weather or threats from other species. However, while our concern here is limited to threats that have their origin in human intentions and actions, the concept can also be used to encompass a wider array of threats to human safety, for example, health threats. In addition, while our focus will be on one particular sub-set of concerns within the governance of security, the conceptual framework we will be developing and exploring has implications for a more comprehensive theoretical framework.

Previously, we referred to our decision to adopt the term 'governance of security' in preference to the more conventional term 'policing'. At this point, it is appropriate to say more about our reasons for adopting that position. In the past, each of us has written about what, in conventional terms, might be called the 'privatisation of policing' or the 'privatisation of social control'. Over the years we have considered issues such as the expansion of commercial security in North America and Europe, the growth of 'mass private property' and the interpenetration of public and private space, the increased transnationalisation of commercial security, the application of private sector principles to public police forces, the relationship between public and private police and the growing salience of 'civil policing' ('self-policing') by citizens in various jurisdictions. Given the focus of that work, our constant emphasis has been to avoid the conflation of policing with the activities of state police, a conflation that had simply been taken for granted in conventional criminological and criminal justice discourse. Contrary to that view, it is clear that policing, far from being the exclusive prerogative of the police, is undertaken by a complex network of public and private agencies. However, despite our repeated efforts to uncouple the terms policing and police, re-conceptualisation has proved difficult. For instance, the Independent Commission on Policing for Northern Ireland (1999) had terms of reference that did not refer explicitly to the Royal Ulster Constabulary but referred instead to 'arrangements for policing'. Despite this, most people who addressed the Commission and its work saw its de facto mandate not as a 'new beginning for policing', in the literal sense of the term, but as a new beginning for the Royal Ulster Constabulary.

This conflation of policing with state police is now restricting our view of what is being done, and what can be done, to govern security under other auspices. In view of that, there are a number of reasons why we opt for the term 'governance of security' rather than for the more conventional term 'policing' – or, indeed, for other terms such as 'the privatisation of policing', the 'hybridisation of policing' or the 'dispersal of social control'. First, while there is undoubtedly a growing recognition of diversity within policing and criminal justice – such recognition being confirmed by the publication of books and articles (both popular and academic) on commercial security, private prisons and the like – that recognition has had minimal impact on a mainstream criminological discourse still preoccupied with issues relating to the administration of security and justice by states. In consequence, those of us whose interests lie in the analysis of diversified networks of security and justice find ourselves increasingly disengaged from the everyday concerns of academic and administrative criminology, and find that we have more in common with those working within non-criminological discourses such as government and politics, social theory, social philosophy, anthropology, ethics and the history of ideas.

Second, while there is undoubtedly some recognition on the part of public police that their historical domination of policing – always, in any case, tenuous – is under threat, that recognition is often grudging. Faced with the growth of corporate governance (from small private security firms carrying out local residential patrols to global companies trading specialised security services in transnational markets) the common police response is a defensive and reactionary one: 'How can we re-impose state police control over policing?'. One of the ideological weapons for attempting to secure that hegemony is, of course, the reduction of the latter to the former. An interesting test case is, at present, under way in Britain following the implementation of the Crime and Disorder Act 1998. That legislation places a statutory duty on local authorities and the police to work together to reduce crime and disorder in their areas. It also requires the probation service, the health authority and the police authority to work with the police and the local authority to develop a crime reduction plan following consultation with the local community. The central plank of this legislation is the formation of local crime reduction partnerships in which local businesses, voluntary agencies, statutory agencies, and members of the local community can be engaged as full participants in the governance of their own security. Whether such genuine partnerships will take root remains to be seen. In the past, similar 'community'-based initiatives have tended to be dominated by the police either because they have successfully maintained their hegemony over policing matters or – more usually – because they have been left to bear the responsibility for implementing the initiatives alone. Whatever the outcome (and one of the preconditions of effective implementation would seem to be an active civic culture – itself a governmental problem), the principles which drive this latest security programme conform with a model of 'networked governance' rather than with one of 'professional police hegemony'. We discuss the issue of community safety and crime reduction partnerships further in Chapter 6.

Third, recognition of the growing diversity of policing, has led some writers to focus less on the restricted concept of police and more on the generic notion of social control. Those adopting this approach would conceive the growth of corporate governance as equivalent to 'the privatization' or 'dispersal' of social control. We have chosen not to deploy this widely-adopted terminology for two crucial reasons. First, the concept of social control is problematic because it takes the primacy of 'the social' for granted. This is an increasingly dubious assumption since, in recent years, 'community' has begun to supplant 'the social' as a governing rationality (Rose, 1996). Second, those who deploy the concept of 'dispersal' almost invariably assume it to indicate a drift towards increased, and therefore ever more pathological, levels of social control. In short, it is assumed that the increased involvement of non-state agencies in the governance of security is, by definition, a 'bad thing' since it increases the sum of such control. By contrast, the position adopted here is that the 'goodness' or 'badness' of programmes for governing security is a function of complex conditions and calculations which cannot be prejudged. In due course, we also contend that while risk-oriented modes of corporate governance pose certain dangers, they also open up new possibilities for security.

To sum up, in writing this book, one of our aims is to keep the distinction between policing and the police constantly in the mind of the reader. Being aware of the difficulty of achieving that, while simultaneously using conventional terminology, we have opted to deploy the language of governance rather than that of policing wherever possible. Sometimes, of course, it has not been possible to do that since the very act of engaging with academic debates tends to force one back into the conventional terminology. Where we have used that terminology, we would simply ask the reader to be mindful of our position. This decision is both a heuristic and strategic one since, by avoiding conventional terminology as much as possible, we deny the assumptions and implications which it imposes on our writing and upon the readers' interpretations of what we have written. (However much we may argue to the contrary, talking about policing always conjures up the image of a public police officer in the readers' mind.) Yet, our decision is not merely a heuristic one. Later, we shall demonstrate that the developments each of us has written about previously – the expansion of commercial and civil policing, the interpenetration of public and private space and so on – are best understood as elements within the wider reconfiguration of contemporary governance.

For now, however, let us make some final observations about the governance of security. Earlier we talked about security programmes and strategies. The strategies that have been developed for governing security have had two central thrusts. The first of these involves responding to threats or breaches of security that have already occurred. The second involves anticipating and seeking to prevent threats that might occur. Of course, more often than not these two approaches are intimately linked; responses to past breaches are often designed in the hope that they will deter future breaches. In this respect, like preventative approaches, they seek to address the future and not just the past. Together these approaches, and the programmes developed to pursue them, constitute the governance of security. In considering these programmes, we will, as was suggested earlier, explore the ways of thinking that underlie them (*mentalities*), the organisational forms used to implement those ways of thinking (*institutions*), the techniques used to turn mentalities into action (*technologies*) and the resulting actions (*practices*).

This framework suggests one critical fact. Nothing that is done to govern security is natural or preordained; different modalities of governance are the product of different applications of human invention. At any time, the governance of security is the result of what people have previously brought into being, and people are constantly re-imagining and re-inventing its forms. In view of this, we are interested in addressing a number of questions. 'What significant changes have occurred in the governance of security?' 'What implications do these changes have for collective life?' 'What new imaginings may be needed to reshape security in any given direction?' 'What ethical factors need to be considered in formulating such new imaginings?' All of these questions, not merely the last, have normative implications. Though our aim is not to promote a particular view of security, we emphasise that security programmes and practices are normative, rather than merely technical, discourses. As such, all who contribute to them have to bear the normative implications of their contributions.

## Developments in the governance of security

Before moving on to a more detailed analysis of these questions, we shall review some key developments in the evolution of the governance of security within Western, and particularly Anglo-American countries. We begin with the development that is usually regarded as fundamental, the development of the 'new police' during and immediately after Sir Robert Peel's tenure as British Home Secretary in the first third of the nineteenth century. Peel's conception of a 'new police' has to be located within a wider security paradigm that has dominated Anglo-American systems over the last two centuries. This paradigm rests on several critical premises. First, the provision of security is perceived to be the responsibility of state governments. Included within this premise is the state's right to define, through lawmaking, those things which are deemed to threaten order. Second, governments exercise their security responsibilities through the employment of specialised professionals, such as police officers, who are endowed with the state's authority. Third, such authority grants agents, like police officers, the legitimate capacity to apply necessary coercion (ultimately through the threat or application of physical force) – by responding to past wrongs and preempting future ones – in order to preserve peace. Fourth, a key element in the governance of security by the state involves apprehending suspected wrongdoers ('offenders'), trying them before a judicial tribunal and punishing them if they are convicted. The exercise of retributive sanctions is intended to achieve several objectives: to re-assert the right moral values; to limit the harm wrong-doers can do; and to dissuade others from committing future wrongs.

Within this broad framework, the governance of security is conceived as a response to collective conflict, or to the threat of collective conflict. This focus on conflict underlies the state's claim to possess a monopoly over the legitimacy of coercion. However, it is important to understand the precise nature of this claim. It does not imply that the state claims a monopoly over the actual exercise of coercion, merely that it claims an exclusive right to determine who may legitimately exercise coercion over others, and in what circumstances. Thus, for instance, the criminal law typically provides that if one private citizen strikes another without the other's consent it is a criminal offence (assault) punishable by the state. If the blow is struck in genuine self-defence, however, and was both 'necessary' and not 'excessive' for that purpose, it will not constitute a criminal offence. Similarly, if a police officer strikes a suspect in the course of a lawful arrest it is not a criminal assault provided the force was 'necessary' in order to effect the arrest, and not 'excessive' in the circumstances. States, it is maintained, need to enjoy such a monopoly in order to fulfil their constitutional responsibilities for the preservation of peace and for the maintenance of order and security in the general public interest. Without such a monopoly, it is argued, the establishment and maintenance of everyone's right to have equal access to security would be impossible. By exercising this monopoly, the state is able to show people the difference between legitimate and illegitimate force and, by so doing, to secure their acquiescence to the state's legitimate authority.

Significantly, the original Peelian conception of the governance of security placed more emphasis on the prevention of disorder than on punitive responses to it, a view expressed in Sir Richard Mayne's 'Instructions' to the Metropolitan Police in 1829:

> It should be understood at the outset that the principal object to be attained is the prevention of crime. To this great end every effort of the police is to be directed. The security of person and property, the preservation of public tranquillity, and all the other objects of a police establishment, will thus be better effected than by the detection and punishment of the offender after he has succeeded in committing the crime . . . When many offences are committed, it must appear to the commissioners that the police is not properly conducted in that division; and the absence of crime will be considered the best proof of the complete efficiency of the police.

Yet, for well over a century state governance of security has been dominated – both in policy and in practice – by a reactive and punitive mentality involving the application of necessary coercion to locate and punish wrongdoers. As we shall explain later, there are understandable reasons why this approach – which we shall call 'the punishment mentality' – has prevailed within state-sponsored security programmes.

However, a second paradigm has also emerged. It is useful to consider how this compares to the previous one which it sometimes supports, sometimes obstructs and sometimes merely works alongside. First, according to the alternative paradigm, security is no longer regarded as the sole, or even the primary, preserve of the state, its governance being exercised under plural auspices. The most significant new authorities to have emerged in this regard have been companies guaranteeing security for particular groups of people, in particular, for their customers and employees. Companies, like states, now act as guarantors of security for particular classes of people occupying particular locations, such as the staff and clients of theme parks and shopping malls. Though these companies typically accept the state's authority and work within the law, they actively define the order to be guaranteed, developing strategies and providing resources for securing that order. While such bodies often work closely with states and their agents, their very existence can be viewed as representing something of a challenge to the first premise of the traditional paradigm, by insisting that states are not the only authorities with the right and capacity to provide guarantees of security.

Second, while these corporate authorities use professional agents to govern security, they usually mix these resources with other non-specialised and non-professional ones. Within this paradigm the provision of security is regarded as 'everybody's business'. Thus, while specialised agents provide professional skills and capacities, they also act as brokers or facilitators who assist in the mobilisation and co-ordination of 'everybody'.

Third, for reasons that we will explore further in subsequent chapters, these private, corporate security programmes commonly reflect a quite different mentality with respect to the governance of security, a mentality that emphasises proactive prevention rather than reactive punishment, and actuarial calculation rather than conventional moral proscription. The result is the development of technologies that bring together very different capacities, moving governance away from a predominant reliance on professionals, whose principle orientation is towards the application of physical force. The knowledge and skills required to govern security are no longer viewed as owned by any particular set of persons or institutions but as widespread. Local, lay knowledge is now regarded as important, indeed as more important, than professional knowledge and capacity. Where the old paradigm seeks to mobilise specialist, often force-based, expertise, the new one seeks to mobilise and integrate a wide spectrum of resources, placing particular emphasis on local knowledge and capacity as a key ingredient in any governance programme.

The corporate emphasis on proactive prevention rather than reactive punishment represents a shift in emphasis from the past to the future. That is, security within corporate settings has become more risk-focused. This focus has a lot to do with the influence of broader business mentalities that require programmes for governing security to submit themselves to the same cost–benefit calculation as other programmes. For example, rather than simply employing a given set of resources to minimise corporate losses, security managers have to articulate their programmes with wider corporate objectives and balance the costs of providing security with the costs of continued loss. However, as we later suggest, this future-oriented approach – what might be termed the 'risk mentality' – is no longer the exclusive preserve of corporate security. On the contrary, state security organisations, such as the police, have become more and more preoccupied with risk-based policies and practices. As we shall see, this is particularly evident in respect of 'problem-oriented' conceptions of policing.

Fourth, whereas authority in the first paradigm depends, ultimately, on the legitimacy of state-granted coercive powers, authority in the second paradigm may be linked to a variety of different auspices. One of these is the authority of contract. For instance, the authority to search library users does not come from the state's legal authority to conduct coercive, non-consensual searches, but from contractual arrangements permitting electronic scanning of those leaving library premises. Such agreements are a condition that libraries impose, as property owners, on those who choose to use their property. While the state can be called upon to use force in support of contracts and their property claims, what is crucial in such settings is that the governance of security is authorised though a variety of different, albeit related, auspices. In that respect, the new paradigm is characterised by its openness to mixed mentalities, auspices and organisational forms. The shift away from physical force with which it is associated, has much to do with its early location in corporate, rather than state, structures. In order for corporations to govern security autonomously and legally, they had to find ways of doing so without falling foul of state claims to monopolise the legitimacy of coercion. This incentive to find ways of operating within state law led corporations to search for ways of governing security that, while not eschewing force entirely, located it more towards the periphery.

As we have just suggested, whereas these features of the governance of security have been particularly evident in corporate settings, they are now becoming increasingly common within state settings as well, the mentalities of the alternative paradigm having begun to penetrate the state sector. The consequence is that we now have two paradigms operating side by side with mentalities and organisational forms becoming intermingled. The particular mix of mentalities and forms varies from setting to setting and, as the mix changes, so do the practices that result. What we find is not only a mixture of auspices but also a mixture of agents (professional and non-professional) and organisational forms (institutions). In short, the governance of security is messier that it once was. Though it is tempting to describe these untidy modes of governance as 'hybrid forms' – a term which one of us has deployed in the past – the very notion of hybridity harks back, somewhat nostalgically, to a world of Platonic ideal forms. However, we need to find ways of thinking beyond the terms of ideals and hybrids. In this book we will use the twin concepts of *networked governance* and *nodal governance* to describe the messier configurations of the present-day governance of security.

## Conclusion

It might be claimed that analysing security through the terminology of governance, rather than through the customary terminology of policing and social control, causes our argument to fall between two stools. On the one hand, it might be said that the approach is too narrow, since institutions like the police are just as much concerned with the provision of justice as they are with the provision of security. On the other hand, it might be said that the approach is too broad since it attempts to reduce a complex of governing strategies (courts, judges, prisons, probation, police, the military, etc.) to a single generic type and, in so doing, denies their specificity.

Let us consider each of these criticisms in turn. There is much to be said for the first point. While some organisations have always concerned themselves exclusively with security matters (military and state security being the obvious examples), civil police forces have always borne the dual mandate of security and justice. Whether such justice is realised in practice, of course, is disputable. Recently, in Britain, there has been much debate about institutionalised racism in the police following disclosure of their incompetence during the investigation of Stephen Lawrence's murder. Yet, leaving such failures aside, police officers are empowered to exercise judicious discretion in the course of their work – something which, at least in the formal sense, is a precondition of justice. In that respect, there has always been an assumption that police are charged with 'doing' both security and justice. Strictly, then, the charge that security fails to encompass some of the functions undertaken by police is correct.

While this argument is historically true, however, the clearly defined separation between security and justice that underpins it – though by no means unimportant – is becoming increasingly difficult to sustain in the contemporary period. One key feature of the emerging risk-based security mentalities described above is their penetration of state police organisations. Another is their tendency to inject risk-based thinking not only into the theory and practice of security but also into the theory and practice of justice. We shall illustrate these developments more fully later. For now, it is sufficient to note that once the distinction between security and justice becomes problematical – by virtue of the impact of risk-based thinking on each – so does the charge that the terminology of governance and security cannot encompass the analysis of contemporary policing. In previous work we have been as guilty of this oversimplification as others. For instance, one of us has contrasted moral and instrumental approaches to the governance of security as two separate ways of governing when it would have been more sensible to conceive of the shift in governance being identified in terms of a re-figuring of instrumental and moral elements.

The second criticism – involving the alleged denial of the specificity of different governing mechanisms – may be given a qualified rejection on similar grounds. It is undoubtedly true that the mentalities, procedures, structures, rules and practices of different institutions – police, probation, courts, the military, the state security services, the social services and the like – are different. It is equally true that recognition of that difference is vital for an understanding of their specific functioning. However, this book is concerned to identify the impact of generic security mentalities on several different institutions – the 'big picture', rather than a range of smaller ones. Admittedly, that approach has inherent dangers. In due course we shall argue that police, probation and social work departments also exhibit many of the facets of risk-based thinking exhibited by corporate agents, such as commercial security companies. Yet, in saying that, we also have to recognise that the impact of these generic developments will vary from location to location. This means that when considering the problems and possibilities inherent in such generic developments we also take account of such specificity and variation.

Finally, a point about the two paradigms described here, one based on punishment, reaction and retribution, the other on risk, anticipation and prevention. Looked at in terms of the 'big picture', our argument is that the governance of security is increasingly oriented around the latter paradigm. However, in practice – the issue of 'specificity' again – it has to be recognised that the two paradigms are in no way mutually exclusive. Thus, in a later chapter, we show how Zero-Tolerance Policing is informed by the old paradigm while, simultaneously, displaying key elements of the new one. This interpenetration of paradigms leads us back to our earlier comment regarding security as a human invention. For in the future, we have not only to consider the problems and possibilities associated with each paradigm but also the desirable balance that, in practice, may need to be struck between them.

In the following chapters we explicate and use the framework outlined here to reflect upon the various re-inventions which have occurred in the governance of security. In the course of doing this we also identify and explore possible future shifts in the governance of security and within governance more broadly. We will use this exposition to focus, in particular, on changes which will contribute to the renewal of two key values associated with democracy: self-direction and self-reliance. Our reasons for focusing on these two values relates to the emerging governmental divide that now separates rich and poor people across the globe.

# 2

# DIMENSIONS OF
# GOVERNANCE

## *(Written with Philip Stenning)*

### Introduction

In Chapter 1 we introduced the general theme of security governance and discussed some of the conceptual and practical issues relating to it. In this chapter, we consider certain general dimensions of governance, an understanding of which will help to inform our later discussion of the changes which have occurred in the governance of security. For that reason the dimensions described here constitute a general framework for thinking about these changes. However, change occurs at different times and to varying degrees across each dimension, so that while general trends may be discernible, the specific pattern of change will vary from place to place, a fact which is as true for the governance of security as it is for other aspects of governance. Later, in Chapters 5 and 6, we shift from the general focus adopted in this chapter and Chapter 1, to a more particular focus. There we shall illustrate, through a consideration of two single cases – recent developments in community policing (Chapter 6) and recent developments in British criminal justice policy (Chapter 7) – how the general dimensions of security governance are mediated by specific empirical conditions.

The present chapter is divided into two sections. In the first section we outline and discuss eight general dimensions of governance. In the second section we identify and comment on two important areas of concern arising from that discussion.

## Eight dimensions of governance

### 1. Who makes the rules?

As we noted in Chapter 1, governance involves reference to some notion of order – a set of explicit or implicit normative prescriptions or rules about the way things ought to be. So, the first key dimension of governance raises the question of who, in a particular collectivity, has the capacity and authority to make the rules that will be treated as the norms of governance. Though this is an empirical question, much of the scholarly discussion of governance has made a priori assumptions about how to answer it. Political scientists and legal centralists, in particular, have considered it axiomatic that the state (through national, regional and local legislatures, executive governments, and their associated laws and regulations) has the monopoly over the authoritative definition of order in a given society. By contrast, anthropologists, legal pluralists and internationalists have long questioned that view. They have maintained that in any given nation or society, a plurality of definitions of order, as well as of authorities which promulgate them, can be discerned, and that often such conceptions of order are in competition or conflict with one another as norms of governance. The making of the rules, in other words, is almost always a matter of contestation and variability related to the fluctuating political economy and social organisation of any particular collectivity, as well as to its relationships with other collectivities.

The spread of neo-liberal ideology in many Western democracies, together with the globalisation trends that have appeared during the last years of the twentieth century, have been accompanied by a discernible shift in the allocation of authority for determining norms of governance. Through these processes, the previously assumed dominance of the state has been challenged not only by alternative, often non-state, authorities but also by supra-state international bodies such as the United Nations, the European Commission and the G7. As a result, state law is no longer the definitive source of norms of governance in particular nation states, either in theory or in practice.

### 2. What is the nature of rules?

Another key dimension of governance concerns the nature of the norms of governance. Specifically, it is important to ascertain two characteristics of such norms: how inclusive are they intended to be? and whose concerns and objectives they are intended to represent? Here, for instance, we may contrast rules that are intended to apply equally to, and represent the concerns and objectives of, every member of a collectivity, with rules which are targetted at, and are intended to represent, only certain members of the collectivity. Public state laws are typically presented as being of the former kind, and the well known notion of the 'rule of law' seeks to capture this inclusiveness as well as the idea that such laws represent some general 'public interest', rather than some more limited private concerns and objectives. By contrast, the rules of private corporate authorities are typically targetted at particular groups (workers, customers, etc.) and are designed to further the private concerns and objectives of the corporate authority.

Presenting the issue in such a dichotomous fashion is, however, misleading. In the first place, it obscures the fact that the distinction between general 'public interests' and specific 'private interests' is by no means clear-cut, and is becoming less and less so as the business of governance becomes more dispersed. Second, it needs to be noted that that there is often a significant disjuncture between stated intention and actual outcome; rules which are presented as being in the general 'public interest' may in fact operate, intentionally or otherwise, in such a way that their effect is highly discriminatory and furthers particular 'private' concerns and objectives over others. Sometimes the discourse of public versus private interests is deployed strategically by governing authorities in an effort to enhance perceptions of their legitimacy, while at the same time obscuring their true purpose. The famous slogan that 'What is good for General Motors is good for America' provides perhaps the most powerful illustration of this phenomenon.

Another important issue concerns the extent to which norms of governance allow for discretion in their implementation. Discretion, especially if it is relatively unfettered, is particularly important because it can provide a means through which an apparently general norm, ostensibly promulgated in the general 'public interest', can in practice be implemented in a discriminatory fashion so that it actually furthers more particular private concerns. As with the question of 'who makes the rules?', the nature of governing norms is always a matter which must be determined empirically rather than through the application of a priori assumptions. In this regard, the empirical observer must pay as much attention to practical outcomes as to discourse.

### 3. What is the focus of governance?

Governance is commonly focused on the future, devising and implementing ways of achieving and maintaining prescribed goals and objectives. However, it also involves responding to problems that may have already arisen, thereby focusing on past events and how to react to them. In the case of the governance of security, this focus on the past – specifically on the issue of how to deal with past 'wrongs' – has been particularly prevalent, being fuelled by notions of retribution, 'just deserts', deterrence and, most importantly, justice. Although the principal focus of punitive responses is to 'right' past 'wrongs', one of their great attractions lies in their claim, simultaneously, to address concerns about the future. Thus, for example, retributive sanctions can be justified both by reference to the past (punishing an offender for a wrongful act) and by reference to the future (using the sanction of punishment as a means of deterring that offender – and other offenders – from committing similar wrongful acts).

While virtually all strategies of governance – especially the governance of security – combine a past and future orientation, overall strategies vary greatly according to how much relative emphasis they place on each. For a variety of reasons – such as a desire not to interfere unduly with the rights to liberty and privacy inscribed in constitutional and legal constraints – the governance of security by state authorities has tended to be dominated by strategies which focus on reacting to past events, relying on these responses as the principal means through which to address future concerns. By contrast, private authorities, relatively free from such formal constraints, more commonly favour proactive strategies, the focus of which is more directly on shaping future behaviour and events.

### 4. Who implements/executes governance?

Just as there is great variability in who 'makes the rules' prescribing order within collectivities, so is it important to identify who is given, or assumes, responsibility for actually achieving compliance with the prescribed order. This involves attention to the agents and institutions of governance. Three characteristics are particularly pertinent in classifying such agents and institutions: their 'public' or 'private' status; the scope (especially the geographic scope) of their authority – which lawyers typically refer to as their 'jurisdiction'; and their status as professionals/experts/specialists or 'lay'/nonexperts/non-specialists. We shall argue, in subsequent chapters, that trends can be discerned in recent years whereby executive responsibility for the governance of security is less likely than before to be concentrated within the hands of professional, expert public officials employed by the state whose jurisdiction extends to the territory of the nation state or some politically defined segment of it, such as a county or municipality. More and more, executive responsibility for the governance of security is being entrusted to, or assumed by, 'private' or non-state agents and institutions, who may be experts or lay persons (e.g. community members or members of Neighbourhood Watch groups), and whose jurisdiction may either be very local (e.g. confined to the territory of a housing estate, gated community or a single institution) or internationally extensive.

It is important to recognise that those who 'make the rules' are typically not the same people or institutions as those who are entrusted with executive responsibility for implementing them. At the level of the state, such 'separation of powers' has, over the centuries, become a matter of constitutional principle in many democracies, and in some there have been attempts to limit the extent to which the executive responsibility for implementation of 'state functions', such as the governance of security, can be entrusted to persons other than 'public' officials. (In Hungary, for example, the constitutions places specific limits on the role of private security.) Nevertheless, implementation of public security laws by private organisations and their employees, and even of private rules by public officials, is increasingly common (Sklansky, 1999).

### 5. Modes of governance

Closely related to the issue of executive responsibility for implementing governance, is the issue of how implementation is achieved. Traditionally, governance has been achieved in quite direct ways; the governing authority establishes (or contracts with) some organisations and authorises their employees to implement or 'enforce' its norms of governance directly on the governed. More recently, however, two important trends away from this traditional model of governance have been discernible in many societies. In the first place, neo-liberal approaches to governance have encouraged a growing separation of the functions of governance, such that while the responsibility for establishing the norms of governance remains with the governing authority, the responsibility for implementing them and securing compliance with them are increasingly devolved to the governed themselves (as individuals or as 'communities'). As Osborne and Gaebler (1993) have described it, drawing on a nautical analogy, government retains the responsibility for 'steering', while the responsibility for 'rowing' is increasingly cast on the citizenry at large. Rose and Miller (1992) have referred to this mode of governance as 'rule at a distance' to distinguish it from the traditional, more direct mode of governance. There is now growing debate, at least in Western industrial democracies, about the trend towards 'governance at a distance' with respect to the governance of security (see e.g. O'Malley, 1992; O'Malley and Palmer, 1996). In later chapters we examine the concept of 'rule at a distance' in detail.

Another important departure from the traditional mode of direct governance of security is the increasingly common practice of 'embedding' the governance of security, both occupationally and functionally (Shearing and Stenning, 1985). Rather than conceiving of the governance of security as the province of a discrete, specialist occupation (such as the police officer or the security guard), there is a growing trend, especially in the private sector, towards embedding security responsibilities within the responsibilities of other occupations. Thus the office receptionist, the retail cashier, the bank teller, the apartment building superintendent and the transit ticket collector can all frequently be found to have responsibilities for security governance included within their job descriptions. Since the retail cashier and the security guard share similar objectives (to make sure that the customer who purchases merchandise leaves the premises having paid for it), responsibility for the two functions of sales and security can be integrated within a single occupation rather than entrusting sales to one employee and security to another.

The governance of security, however, is often 'embedded' in another way through the practice of designing security features into the built environment – a practice made increasingly feasible as a result of significant advances in security technology. The governance of security through such means is very direct, but does not require dedicated human agency. Rather, the environment is built to restrict the possibility of non-compliance with security requirements either by eliminating that possibility entirely or by making it much more difficult and/or risky. Consider, for example, the apparently mundane issue of seating design in public places. Davis (1990) describes how, during the 1980s, the city authorities in

Los Angeles introduced public benches with spherical seating, thereby encouraging people to 'move along' through public space and, more importantly, deterring homeless people from trying to sleep on benches. Commuters on London Underground's Jubilee Line will note that the seats installed on platforms (narrow, sloped and raised high off the ground) are designed for a similar purpose – 'short-term leaning' rather than 'long-term resting'.

## 6. Processes of governance

Governance may be achieved consensually or through coercion or, to put it another way, it may be imposed unilaterally or achieved through agreement following some kind of negotiation. Political and civil governance tends to favour negotiation over imposition, while judicial governance (especially through the criminal law) relies much more heavily on coercion and imposition. Commonly, however, strategies of governance involve some blend of the two approaches – an initial attempt to achieve compliance through consent or negotiation, with imposition threatened should consensus not be achievable. Since governance through consent is generally cheaper, more pleasant, less socially disruptive and divisive, and less dangerous (for the governors and the governed), it is not surprising that it is often the preferred option, with coercive imposition being regarded as an option of last resort. Indeed, the laws of many states require such an approach (e.g. by requiring police to demand submission before using lethal force except in extreme situations and by providing, in theory at least, sanctions against the use of 'excessive' force by state officials).

Strategies for the governance of security may thus be differentiated according to how much relative emphasis is placed on achieving compliance through coercion or the threat of coercion, or through negotiation and consent. In the case of governance of security under private auspices, less overtly coercive processes are commonly resorted to in the light of legal sanctions against resort to more overtly coercive means of governance. Arrangements for security are often arrived at through processes of negotiation (such as collective bargaining in the workplace or contractual arrangements), although these are often backed up by the possibility of more coercive processes should consent and compliance not be forthcoming. There are, of course, exceptions to this rule. A century ago, organisations like the Pennsylvania Coal and Iron Police – the notorious and brutal 'Pennsylvania Cossacks' – acted as private armies on behalf of industrialists when state authorities abrogated responsibility for the regulation of industrial relations (Bowden, 1978). Nevertheless, as many scholars (e.g. Bittner, 1991) have emphasised, the threat and symbols of physical force typically figure more prominently in the governance processes of the state than in those of the corporate sector.

## 7. Technologies of governance

Closely related to modes and processes of governance are the tools or technologies which are deployed to achieve it. Like plumbers or carpenters, those who execute the governance of security require appropriate tools for the job. Although many physical tools (such as guns, batons, handcuffs, vehicles, surveillance devices, etc.) are commonly required for the governance of security, security personnel also rely on legal tools (powers of arrest, search, seizure, etc.), symbolic tools (such as the public respect and deference which the police officer or the police organisation enjoys) (Loader, 1997; Mopas and Stenning, 2000) and personal tools (such as personal physique, strength, charisma, communication skills, etc.) to achieve compliance with security requirements. The contents of this security 'tool kit' (Stenning, 2000) vary significantly between different kinds of security personnel (e.g. public police officers, private security officers, border guards, etc.), and even among similar personnel depending on such factors as age, years of job experience, gender, attitude towards the job, etc. And there is every reason to believe that the use which any individual officer makes of the tools available to him or her in doing security work varies during the course of his or her career.

Equally importantly, different modes and processes of security governance require different tools, and combinations of tools, for their effective achievement. A strategy of security governance such as the currently popular 'community-based policing', for instance, which emphasises negotiation, co-operation and consent in the achievement of compliance, can be expected to place greater emphasis on such personal tools as communication skills and personal charisma, and on some civil and administrative law powers (Fischer, 1998), than on the more overtly coercive tools such as guns, batons and criminal law powers commonly required with 'law enforcement'-focused strategies such as 'zero tolerance policing'. In most jurisdictions, the tools available to private sector personnel – especially those associated with physical coercion – are restricted by state laws, which in turn encourages resort to less overtly coercive processes of security governance.

While the modes and processes of security governance thus influence the tools that are chosen, the reverse may sometimes be true. The old adage that 'to a person with a hammer everything begins to look like a nail' may have some applicability in this context, and is perhaps reflected in concerns, for instance, that the tools most commonly associated with public police may have the effect of attracting aggressive, authoritarian people to the job, which in turn shapes the culture of the police organisation, the way the job is perceived and how it is done. By the same token, of course, should police employ alternative technologies, the effect on recruitment, culture and practice might be significant. Later, we consider whether the police's increased deployment of 'problem-oriented' and 'risk-based' technologies might have a positive impact in these areas.

## 8. Mentalities of governance

Probably the most significant dimension of governance, however, is the mentality that is brought to the task. A mentality is a mental framework that shapes the way we think about the world and, as a result, the way we react to the situations and circumstances we encounter in our daily lives. It sets the terms within which our perceptions and thoughts are constructed and translated into action. Mentalities are more often implicit than explicit, however, and must often be inferred from the actions that flow from them. Generally, we act not because we have consciously thought through and adopted a mentality that promotes that particular action, but because we constantly use methods (often embedded in habits) that imply that mentality or practical reasoning. We typically adopt these methods without thinking much about the mentality they imply. What we tend to think about are practical concerns, such as finding methods that enable us to do something. As this implies, a common reason for adopting our methods is that we believe they are a requirement of competency. We use the methods we do because they define us as competent people.

But these methods of governance, for whatever reason we may adopt them, implicitly reflect a mentality. This way of thinking can be relatively contained in the sense that it is only linked to the techniques in question. However, it can, and often does, become more widespread. This happens because mentalities, unlike methods and practices, are not situationally specific. So when we enact a mentality by choosing a particular technique in particular circumstances, it often infiltrates other areas of our life. When it does so it contributes to our identities more generally – it shapes a broader consciousness.

A number of quite different mentalities of governance – punishment, risk management, harm reduction and remedial/restorative approaches – have come to be associated with the governance of security. In Chapters 3 and 5 we consider, respectively, the punishment mentality and the mentality of risk. For the moment it is sufficient to point out that the mentality which underlies a particular approach to the governance of security has implications for, and influences on, most of the other dimensions of governance discussed in this chapter. Thus, for instance, security governance based on the punishment mentality tends to entail a principal focus on past events, an emphasis on physical coercion, a direct mode of governance through discrete, collectively-sponsored institutions and an imposed rather than negotiated process prescribed through generally applicable rules intended to promote some collective interests. A punishment regime that does not display these characteristics may run the risk of losing legitimacy and being charged with vigilantism. By contrast, the risk management mentality favours an emphasis on embedded modes of 'governance at a distance', focused on the future, and achieved through processes of situationally-specific negotiation which privilege the use of less overtly coercive tools of governance and often involve non-expert, 'lay' persons in their implementation.

As we shall illustrate in subsequent chapters, however, it would be a serious mistake to suppose that the different dimensions of governance are aligned with their 'corresponding' mentalities in a neat and orderly fashion. In fact, at the empirical level, the picture is far more complicated, 'pure forms' being the exception rather than the rule.

## Issues for consideration

The eight general dimensions of governance just outlined will inform our argument at various points throughout this book. To conclude this chapter we comment, briefly, on two issues arising from the previous discussion, each of which is explored more fully in later chapters.

## *The public and the private*

Our discussion so far has referred to, but glossed over, the distinction between 'public' and 'private' authorities, places, concerns and objectives and personnel. Early analysts of private security governance sought to explain the respective roles of public and private security providers by reference to the geographical domains in which they worked. The security of public places, it was argued, is essentially the responsibility of public authorities, and is to be undertaken in the 'public interest', while the role of private security providers is confined to the protection of private property in the interest of its owners. While this explanation may have been true at some early stage of the development of private security provision, it has proved increasingly difficult to defend as a generalisation for two main reasons. First, and most obviously, the role of public security providers is not confined to the governance of security in public places. Although one of their principal strategies – routine patrol – occurs in public places (i.e. the streets), their mandate requires them to respond to crime, both reactively and preventively, wherever it may occur. For that reason they are given special legal powers to enter private property in order to fulfil this mandate (Stinchcombe, 1963). Indeed, in the last quarter of the twentieth century, their capacity and authority to penetrate private property and to intrude on private relationships has been enhanced through advances in technology (e.g. wiretaps) and through enabling legislation, even in liberal democratic states (Marx, 1988).

Second, and less obviously, during the last thirty or forty years an important change has occurred in the character of property, especially that contained within urban areas. As a result of that change it can no longer be assumed that private property is necessarily located in private places. On the contrary, many places to which members of the public have routine access are found on property, which is privately owned. Such places, which have been referred to in the literature as examples of 'mass private property' (Shearing and Stenning, 1981; Jones and Newburn, 1998: 46–51, 104–14), include venues such as shopping malls, housing estates, sports stadia, amusement parks and other recreational facilities. These locations cannot easily be placed within the conventional conceptual framework of 'public or private' since, although they are privately owned, they are shared by communities (of residents, workers, customers and the like) who live, work, trade and play in them – they constitute what might be thought of as a 'new commons' (Von Hirsch and Shearing, 2000) or new 'communal spaces' (Hermer *et al.*, 2002). In that sense they have a marked public character. Despite that public character, however, many of these locations are privately owned, often by large corporations. In such places – which may comprise a significant proportion of the totality of 'public space' in many urban environments – private authorities may assume the governance of security either primarily or exclusively (Sklansky, 1999). The result is that more and more security governance in public places is undertaken privately, thus calling further into question conventional explanations of the distinction between the roles of public and private authorities (Bayley and Shearing, 1996)

One result of these developments has been to call into question attempts to draw a clear line between the roles, responsibilities, functions and tasks of public and private authorities in the governance of security within liberal democratic states (see e.g. Home Office, 1995; Independent Committee of Inquiry, 1996). Those attempts have been further undermined by the growing influence of neo-liberal and post-modern re-configurations of the state's role (Rose and Miller, 1992; O'Malley and Palmer, 1996; Garland, 1996; Rose, 1996). Thus, the rationalisations which mobilise individuals, organisations and communities to bear greater and greater responsibility for their own safety and security – 'responsible citizenship' (Johnston, 1992b), citizen 'responsibilisation' (Garland, 1996) 'community policing' and 'partnership' to name but a few – indicate that the state's traditional role as exclusive guarantor of security has been superseded by new public–private, or better, state–non-state networks. It is notable that the British government's crime plan for the next ten years, *Criminal Justice: The Way Ahead* (Home Office, 2001a) promises experimental accreditation of private security staff, working under police co-ordination, to deliver improved community safety. Drawing upon the experience of 'civil guards' in the Netherlands, the British government has also put substantial investment into schemes for the provision of 'neighbourhood' or 'community' wardens in many municipalities (Jacobson and Saville, 1999; Donaldson and Johnston, 2001).

It is now virtually impossible to identify any function within the governance of security in democratic states that is not, somewhere and under some circumstances, performed by non-state authorities as well as by state ones. As a result, policy-makers are now more ready to accept that the effective governance of security requires co-operation, collaboration and 'networking' between partners and that exact demarcation between the respective responsibilities of partners may be difficult, or even impossible, to establish (Greene *et al.*, 1995; Bayley and Shearing, 1996; Jones and Newburn, 1998; Kempa *et al.*, 1999; Loader, 2000). Indeed, the key issue for the future will not be demarcation of functions, but effective co-ordination of networks. Significantly, that is one of the main conclusions of the British government's ten-year crime plan:

> There has always been a wide range of people contributing to community safety in various forms. These include park keepers (some with constabulary powers), security guards in shopping centres, car park attendants, neighbourhood wardens, night club bouncers and the private security industry. The issue for policing is how these various activities can be coordinated to make the most effective contribution to making safer communities.
>
> (Home Office, 2001a)

It is, therefore, vital that we understand the shifts which have occurred, and which continue to occur, in security governance in order that a rational foundation for policy decisions in this area can be established.

### Governance, regulation and the state

A second issue, to which we shall return in later chapters, concerns the role of the state under conditions of dispersed governance. Three decades ago cutting-edge criminological theory grappled with 'the problem of the state'. At that time, the particular 'problem' in question was considered to be the state's oversight of a legal process and a criminal justice system that, together, acted on behalf of the rich and powerful, and discriminated systematically against the poor and weak. The mood of this period was well captured in the demand for a radical criminology whose object was 'to show up the law, in its true colours, as the instrument of the ruling class . . . and [to show] that rule makers are also the greatest rule-breakers' (Taylor *et al.*, 1975: 89). According to that view, while the state – through the law – presented itself as an independent adjudicator between competing interests and claimed to ensure that all individuals had equal access to justice, formal legal equality was, in reality, a sham. For radical writers the state justice system was primarily a vehicle for the delivery of oppression, discrimination and inequity.

Thirty years later, the cutting edge of criminological theory has shifted from the highly structured world of radical Marxism to the destructured world of Foucauldian scholarship. Yet, that shift also reveals a strange paradox. At one level, little seems to have changed since many of today's theorists still appear to be grappling with 'the problem of the state'. At another level, much has changed since the problem they are grappling with has been transformed beyond all recognition. Thirty years ago the state was considered to *be* 'the problem', its capitalist character rendering it structurally incapable of representing general 'public interests' over particular private ones. Today, the 'problem' is conceived very differently. Now, it is argued, neo-liberalism has disaggregated the state apparatus, depriving it of its capacity to represent 'public interests' adequately in a fragmented and market-dominated society. One proposed solution is a 're-configuring [of] the linkage between policing and the state' in order to ensure that security can be re-constituted as a public good (Loader and Walker, 2001: 9). The difference between these two definitions of 'the problem of the state' is striking, the former seeing the state as a fundamental obstacle to the representation of public interests, the latter seeing it as a necessary precondition for such representation. In effect, during a thirty-year period, the state has been transformed from 'problem' to (part) 'solution'.

The question of the state's future role in security governance is, undoubtedly, a complex one. There are those who would try to define that role in precise functional terms. Garland (1996), for example, has argued that a distinction should be drawn between 'the *punishment* of crime, which remains the business of the state (and . . . a significant symbol of state power) and the *control* of crime, which is increasingly deemed to be "beyond the state" in significant respect' (Garland, 1996: 459: emphasis in original). Garland contends that, whereas the state might willingly disperse power through strategies of 'responsibilisation' in respect of crime control, it is not particularly good at 'acting at a distance' in respect of punishment. On the contrary, he suggests, the shift towards increasingly harsh regimes of punishment in many liberal democratic states is indicative of a re-assertion of state power. However, one should be sceptical of such neat functional distinctions for two reasons. First, claims about the inherent functional boundaries of state power have been made, with equal conviction, in the past and have, subsequently, been exposed as faulty. Two decades ago, Cohen argued that while the private sector might supplant the state in some areas of activity *'this would be an impossible outcome in crime control.* For the state to give up here would be to undercut its very claim to legitimacy' (1983: 117: emphasis added). The fact that developments in the last two decades have demonstrated the error of this prediction – and in another two decades may demonstrate the error of Garland's – suggests the need to exercise caution in this regard. Second, a central argument of this book will be that the 'good governance' of security and justice (or, in Garland's terms, 'crime control' and 'punishment') demand the effective integration – rather than the functional differentiation – of the two, an issue we discuss at length in Chapter 8.

One thing that requires consideration in respect of the state's role in the furtherance of good security governance is the issue of regulation. Though neo-liberal ideologues railed at the alleged bureaucratic excesses of the Keynesian welfare state, the practices which neo-liberalism sanctioned, such as market competition, privatisation and dispersed governance led, ironically, to the massive expansion of regulatory regimes. Thus, the outright privatisation of some public services (such as gas, water and transport), the partial privatisation of others (such as prisons) and the 'marketisation' of many more (such as universities and the police) coincided with the birth of a 'new regulatory state' (Braithwaite, 2000). Of course, the concept of a 'new regulatory state' fits neatly with Osborne and Gaebler's (1993) view that the state now concentrates on the 'steering' functions of governance, leaving the responsibility of 'rowing' to other, more dispersed, agents. However, this view is, undoubtedly, simplified since at the global level – though by no means only there – transnational bodies have responsibility not just for the regulation of business corporations, but also for the regulation of states themselves. In that regard, it is important to recognise the state as both *regulator* and *regulated,* a dual status which, among other things, problematises the attempt to conceive it as the exclusive locus of public interests.

We shall explore these issues further in due course. For the moment, let us merely make three observations. First, we are unconvinced by those who, while mindful that the state's monopoly of governance is at an end, appear to postulate the need for a state monopoly of regulation. Second, while we would recognise the negative effects of unregulated market forces in the governance of security and accept that the state has an important role to play in minimising those negative effects, we would also argue that certain private modes of governance offer benefits which state governance has been unable to match and avoid disbenefits which state governance has been unable to avoid. Third, we would argue that the solution to the problem of security governance lies neither in the autonomy of the market nor in the imposition of state regulation over the market but in a 'nodal security synthesis' whereby the state checks community and market failure and the community/market check state failure. We outline this argument in Chapter 8.

## Conclusion

Our identification of the eight dimensions of governance has served two functions. First, it has provided a general reference point for some of the specific conceptual issues raised about security governance in Chapter 1. There, we claimed that programmes and strategies aiming to guarantee security typically involve six elements. First, they require stipulations about which activities should be permitted and which activities proscribed; in other words, a view of what security entails. The issues of rulemaking, the nature of rules and the processes of contestation involved in governance (dimensions 1–3) are particularly germane to this topic. A second requirement is the existence of state, corporate or communal authorities seeking to offer guarantees of security. Our analysis of the execution/implementation of decisions and of the processes of 'dispersal' and 'embedding' of practices (dimensions 4–5) is especially pertinent to this issue. In addition to these, four further elements are implicit in security programmes and strategies: the deployment of specific technologies (dimension 7); the availability of institutional support (dimensions 4 and 6); and the presence of particular mentalities (dimension 8), all of which condition the nature of the resulting security practices. In this chapter we have demonstrated how these elements are a generic feature of govern-ance as well as a specific property of security governance.

Second, the eight dimensions identified in this chapter provide a framework for understanding the key changes in security governance that are the focus of this book. As we shall illustrate in the remaining chapters, the governance of security in contemporary societies has been changing along each of these dimensions though not in precisely the same way or at precisely the same pace everywhere. Understanding the implications of these changes for security governance in the twenty-first century requires the recognition that some long-accepted analytical distinctions in the literature, such as that between 'public' and 'private' spheres, are increasingly problematic as conceptual underpinnings for debate and analysis. We have identified mentalities of governance as the most crucial of these dimensions of governance, shaping and influencing, as they do, most of the other dimensions. It is to these mentalities of governance that we now turn.

# 3

# THE PUNISHMENT MENTALITY AND COERCIVE TECHNOLOGIES

## Introduction

In Chapter 2 we suggested that the punishment mentality is focused primarily, though by no means exclusively, on past events, emphasises coercive physical force, involves direct governance through the state and consists of an imposed process prescribed through general rules. Cohen's account of 'the punitive style of control' reflects this view:

> . . . it entails the infliction of pain (loss, harm, suffering); it must always identify an individual held responsible for the breaking of abstract rules (notably legal rules); it is moralistic in essence; it is coercive rather than voluntary and (an important feature to which we will return) it involves the transfer of social control functions to a third party – that is, the deviance or conflict is removed from the parties concerned (for example, victim and offender) and handed over to a specialised agency (usually the state's criminal justice system).
>
> (1994: 67–8)

This punitive model has so dominated debate in criminal justice that it has come to be regarded as the paradigmatic form of security governance – a key component (along with periodic doses of 'welfare' and 'treatment') of what Feeley and Simon have termed 'the Old Penology'.

> . . . the Old Penology is rooted in a concern for individuals, and preoccupied with such conceptions as guilt, responsibility and obligation, as well as diagnosis, intervention

and treatment of the individual offender. It views committing a crime a deviant or antisocial act which is deserving of a response, and one of its central aims is to ascertain the nature of the responsibility of the accused and hold the guilty responsible.

(1994: 173)

In this chapter we consider the role of punishment in the governance of security and justice. The chapter is divided into two sections. First we examine the punishment mentality. In doing this we focus on Beccaria's 'classical' model and consider some of the moral and instrumental justifications that are put forward for punishment. We also examine the interaction between that mentality and the classical institutions of punishment, the product of which was a 'neo-classical' compromise. The second section explores the role of coercive force as a technology of governance.

## The punishment mentality and institutions of punishment

### *Justifying punishment*

Punishment, not least when it is imposed by the state, requires moral justification. The reason for this is obvious. Locking people up, hanging, flogging or fining them, involves the infliction of something unpleasant – physical or mental pain, social disapproval, social isolation, the deprivation of liberty and suchlike. It is, therefore, incumbent on the governing authority to provide some justification for such infliction. Punishment is, in other words, a moral issue:

> Punishment requires justification because it is morally problematic. It is morally problematic because it involves doing things to people that (when not described as 'punishment') seem morally wrong. [Thus] it is usually wrong to lock people up, to take their money without return, or put them to death.
>
> (Duff and Garland, 1994: 2)

Theories of punishment are usually classified in one or other of two ways. Consequentialist (or 'forward-looking') theories maintain that the rightness or wrongness of an action depends on its consequences. An action with good consequences is deemed to be right. One with bad consequences is deemed to be wrong. In order to justify a system of punishment, then, we must demonstrate that it does some good and that no alternative system could do as much good with as little cost. All consequentialist accounts are, therefore, 'forward-looking', justifying particular punishments by their alleged future consequences. Usually, consequentialists justify punishment by its instrumental contribution to some desired end (such as crime prevention, security, welfare or happiness). The main criticism of consequentialism is that it might be used to justify manifestly unjust punishments (such as draconian punishments against the guilty or scapegoating of the innocent) in the name of 'good consequences'.

By contrast, non-consequentialist or deontological ('backward-looking') theories claim that actions may be deemed right or wrong according to their intrinsic character, irrespective of their consequences. According to this view, punishment is justified, not because of its alleged future (instrumental) consequences, but because it is deemed to be an appropriate response to a past event (the offence). In this case the justification for punishment is considered to be its inherent 'rightness' vis-à-vis the (past) offence, rather than any future (deterrent or other) value it might possess.

Clearly, the latter approach is associated with retributively punitive and 'just deserts' models of justice. Those who justify punishment in terms of just deserts and/or retribution argue that offenders deserve punishment because it is an appropriate response to the wrong which has been committed. Here, the justification is retrospective: people should be punished because they have already (in the past) committed a wrongful act. Thus, for the retributionist, any consideration of the future consequences of the sanction (for example, that it might deter people from future wrong-doing) is either irrelevant or peripheral. For some deontologists the moral justification for the imposition of punitive sanctions is equivalent to the principle of *lex tallonis* ('an eye for an eye'). For others, the justification may be more complex. A particularly interesting approach is the one taken by British criminologist Patricia Morgan who conceives the exercise of punishment as, itself, an expression of morality:

> [Punishment aims] to re-assert the seriousness of certain moral rules of a community . . . Punishment in its pure sense is not *in order* to get people in future to obey a moral rule: it

is an expression of that rule itself. It is, therefore, mistaken to ask 'What is punishment for'? unless one is prepared to ask the same question about morality.

(Morgan, 1978)

Deontologists usually advocate a range of punishments of different degrees of severity which are, in turn, related to crimes with different degrees of seriousness. This approach has certain obvious strengths and weaknesses (Cavadino and Dignan, 1997). On the one hand, it treats 'like' cases (those considered to be equally deserving of a given punishment) similarly; and since only punishment of the guilty is justified, it avoids the consequentialist danger of punishing the innocent for 'good' instrumental reasons or punishing the guilty excessively on the grounds that this will deter others. On the other hand, unlike instrumental or utilitarian approaches, retributive ones are sometimes justified entirely emotively and, as a result, some critics maintain that retribution is merely vengeance by another name.[1]

'Backward-looking' approaches are associated with the imposition of punitive sanctions. By contrast, 'forward-looking' (consequentialist) approaches may be invoked to justify either punitive or welfare-based sanctions or, indeed – as is commonplace – some combination of each. Consequentialism justifies sanctions according to their alleged future consequences. For the consequentialist, the infliction of sanctions is likely to reduce wrongdoing more than would be the case if none were to be imposed. In practice, claims about the reductive capacity of sanctions are sustained by reference to two main principles: deterrence and reform. The first involves claims about the alleged deterrent effect of punishment. In this case the claim is two-fold. On the one hand, it is said that individuals who experience punishment find it so unpleasant that they desist from further wrongdoing. On the other hand, it may also be said that the infliction of punishment on individuals acts as a general deterrent for the rest of us, steering us away from the commission of wrongful acts. The second involves claims about the reformative and rehabilitative effects of (either punitive or welfare-based) sanctions on the offender. Consider an example of the use of punitive sanctions for reformative ends. In 1779 the Penitentiary Act was passed permitting the construction of two penitentiaries in London. Though these were never built, similar institutions were developed in other parts of the country. Sir George Paul, the instigator of the Gloucester Penitentiary, had a clear conception of how the regime would work as a 'total institution'. Prisoners were to wear uniforms and have their heads shaved – ostensibly to prevent disease but, in reality, as a form of what George called 'mortification' (killing off the old identity). Authority in the penitentiary was to be rigid. Guards were to be impersonal. The prisoner, isolated from the outside world would, it was anticipated, be reformed through hard work and contemplation. Subsequent to this there was also a major debate about the alleged reformative benefits of 'silent' or 'solitary' regimes. Coldbath Fields was one of twenty prisons which banned all speech and gesture, while Pentonville kept prisoners in solitary cells for up to eighteen months at a time in order to effect their reform (Ignatieff, 1978).

Alternatively, reform may be perceived as a process of 'rehabilitation through welfare/treatment'. The rationale for this approach grew out of nineteenth-century positivistic criminology and had a major impact on the development of the 'therapeutic' regimes that prevailed for much of the first two-thirds of the twentieth century. During the 1920s in the USA 'Progressives' argued in favour of the rehabilitation of offenders and influenced policy-makers to introduce such reforms as probation, parole and indeterminate sentencing (Lilley *et al.*, 1989). A similar pattern of events unfolded in Britain during the early twentieth century. There, the culmination of that process was the 1969 Children and Young Persons Act which, among other things, stipulated that 10–13-year-old offenders should be dealt with by 'care' rather than by criminal proceedings, and which abolished Attendance Centres and Borstals, replacing them with 'intermediate treatment centres' (Hughes, 1998)

### The 'Classical' mentality of punishment

Forward and backward-looking arguments constitute ideal types that are seldom realised in pure form in proposals for governance. They are typically combined. What distinguishes these proposals is the way in which forward and backward looking elements are combined. To explore this we turn to an enduring rationality for integrating these conceptions of governance that was persuasively articulated in the eighteenth century. Though we shall make further references to the welfare-based model later in this and subsequent chapters, for now we shall concentrate on the 'Classical' version of the punishment mentality. This version was propounded by Cesare Beccaria whose book *On Crimes and Punishments* was first published in 1764. In discussing Beccaria's position, one thing should be noted from the outset. While the backward-looking approach to punishment is exclusively oriented to the provision of justice, the forward-looking approach – as exemplified in Beccaria's work – is oriented *both to the provision of justice and to the provision of security*. This attempt to integrate security and justice within a single mentality is based upon the view that punishment has a dual capacity: to right past wrongs and to prevent future ones. While Beccaria's objective – to integrate security and justice within a single mentality is a laudable one – we propose, in the final chapter, an alternative mode of integration that does not draw upon the punishment paradigm. First, however, let us review the main elements of Beccaria's position.

In eighteenth-century Europe, punishment was dominated by capital and corporal sanctions. In addition to the physical severity of penalties, there was no due process, and judicial discretion ensured that justice was a lottery, the innocent being as much in danger of sanction as the guilty. In Beccaria's view this system was highly inefficient at controlling crime. The system he proposed to replace it with was based upon alternative principles: that due process should obtain; that punishment should be certain and regular; that fixed penalties, proportionate to the seriousness of the offence, should be put into place; that penalties should only be severe enough to deter future wrongdoing; and that all people should be regarded as having full responsibility for their actions and, as such, that all forms of clemency or mitigation should be expunged from judgement.

Beccaria's argument is predicated upon the existence of a social contract between the governing authority and the governed where the latter are prepared to sacrifice some liberty in pursuit of utilitarian principles. However, the fact that people are rational and selfish, Beccaria maintained, causes them to hedge their acceptance of the contract with a qualification. The simple fact is, he suggests, that since all rational individuals can imagine themselves doing wrong, they will only countenance the state having the right to punish sufficiently to deter offenders from further wrongdoing. Disproportionate punishment is, therefore, deemed to be unacceptable since rational individuals will never countenance the prospect of subjecting themselves to excessive punishments. More than that, however, excessive punishments cause crime since, by making minor and serious crimes equally punishable, they encourage would-be offenders to commit more serious offences: 'If an equal punishment be ordained for two crimes that injure society in different degrees, there is nothing to deter men from committing the greater as often it is attended with greater advantage' (Beccaria, 1764: chapter 6, Of the Proportion Between Crimes and Punishments). For that reason, Beccaria's opposition to capital punishment was based on utilitarian reasons (its inefficiency as a sanction) rather than on humanitarian ones. The same utilitarian reasons explain why he was happy to promote both corporal punishment and public humiliation for the deterrence of certain types of crimes. His promotion of public humiliation, for instance, rested upon its alleged utility as a general deterrent with the capacity to inspire terror in the spectator as well as in the sufferer.

In Beccaria's view, physical sanctions, such as corporal punishment, social isolation or public humiliation, were not intended to torment the body, however much they might do so. Rather, punishments were to be directed at the minds of rational subjects, albeit through the vehicle of their bodies (Roshier, 1989).

> The end of punishment . . . is no other than to prevent the criminal from doing further injury to society and to prevent others from committing the like offence. Such punishments, therefore, and such a mode of inflicting them, ought to be chosen as will make the strongest and most lasting impressions on the minds of others, with the least torment to the body of the criminal.
>
> (Beccaria, 1764: chapter 12,
> Of the Intent of Punishments)

The overriding objective of punishment is, therefore, to bring about the efficient control of crime. For that reason, Beccaria, like deontologists but for different reasons, contends that the punishment should be proportional to the crime though, unlike them, he insists that proportionality should relate, not to the sinfulness of the act, but to the harm it inflicts on society:

> It is not only in the common interest of mankind that crime should not be committed, but that crimes of every kind should be less frequent, in proportion to the evil they produce to society. Therefore the means made use of by the legislature to prevent crimes should be more powerful in proportion as they are destructive of the public safety and happiness, and as the inducements to commit them are

stronger. Therefore there ought to be a fixed proportion between crimes and punishments.

(Beccaria, 1764: chapter 6,
Of the Proportion Between Crimes and Punishments)

Beccaria identifies two further critical aspects of punishment. First, it should be certain: 'the certainty of even a mild punishment will make a bigger impression than the fear of a more awful one' (Beccaria, 1764: chapter 27, Of the Mildness of Punishments). Second, it should be prompt: 'the smaller the lapse of time between the misdeed and the punishment, the stronger and more lasting the association in the human mind between the ideas *crime* and *punishment*' (Beccaria, 1764: chapter 19, Of the Advantage of Immediate Punishment). Since it is vital to make connections between crime and punishment in the mind of the subject, Beccaria is also keen to establish symbolic 'associations' between crimes and the punishments considered most appropriate to them: fines for property crimes; corporal punishment for violence; banishment for disturbance of the public tranquillity, and so on.

To sum up, Beccaria's argument is premised upon rational individuals living under a social contract. His intent is to replace arbitrary justice with a new 'calculus' of calibrated punishments. According to this calculus, excessive punishment is deemed ineffective on grounds of utility, the sole object of punishment being to prevent crime through deterrence. Two key principles underlie the judicial process. On the one hand, mitigation and clemency are denied because punishment has to be proportional to the social harm done by the act. (Allowing mitigation to poor, homeless or psychotic offenders would not only deny the rational offender's free choice, it would break the link between utility and punishment.) On the other hand, proportionate sentences backed by due process, ensure the inalienable right of individuals to 'walk free' once they have received their punishment.

### The 'neoclassical compromise'

So far, we have outlined the principles that underpin the classical paradigm of punishment. The reader will note that the paradigm conforms more or less exactly with Cohen's (1994) definition of 'the punitive style of control' since it entails the infliction of pain; holds individuals responsible for the breaking of abstract legal rules; is moralistic (if not in the deontologist sense, at least in the sense that the social contract upon which classical punishment is predicated implies the existence of some moral community); and assumes the existence of a specialised body of criminal justice officials able and willing to apply the calculus of punishment contained in the model.

But what of that process of application? At the end of Chapter 2 we suggested that while mentalities shape perceptions and are inscribed in methods, they do not necessarily align with their 'corresponding' technologies and practices. On the contrary, the relationship between mentalities, the institutions with which they interact, and the technologies and practices which arise from that interaction may be complex and unstable. This is borne out in the present example, the implementation of the classical model having proved decidedly problematical. There were a number of reasons for this. For one thing, utilitarian writers like Bentham, while committed to the principle of preventive and proportionate punishment, had little time for offenders having the right to 'walk free', and advocated, instead, that they should be 'reformed' by alternative institutional means, such as the prison. The implication of this was that effective reform might require indeterminate sentences and a quite different assemblage of penal institutions from that demanded by Beccaria. For another, Beccaria's requirement that there should be proportionality between offence and punishment, regardless of the background and circumstances of the offender, conflicted with the judiciary's demand for discretion in sentencing. The resulting compromise with judicial institutions gave rise to a 'neoclassical' resolution: 'a retention of the assumption of free will, but with an allowance that it is sometimes freer than at other times and that proportionality of punishments should be adjusted to these varying degrees of freedom' (Roshier, 1989: 10). In effect, neoclassicism provided the basis for the modern Western criminal justice system we know today, a variety of factors (age, mental capacity, intent, etc.) being invoked to minimise or maximise the culpability of offenders and to gauge the extent to which they could be held responsible for their actions. This approach was, of course, further validated by the growing influence of positivist criminologists whose suggestion that biological, psychological or social factors might mediate between the offender and the offence, gave credence to the view that some actions might be environmentally conditioned rather than the product of unimpaired rational choice.

This experience confirms that the relationship between mentalities, institutions, technologies and practices of punishment is a complex one. But we need to be clear about the nature of that complexity. Our argument is not merely that Beccaria's 'pure' classical version of the punishment mentality was undermined by a combination of recalcitrant criminal justice institutions and positivist intellectual influences to produce, first, a neoclassical compromise, and later, the therapeutic–rehabilitative model of justice which prevailed for much of the twentieth century. That such a shift – sometimes described as a shift from punishment to welfare – occurred may be true, but it obscures two fundamental continuities which need to be emphasised.

The first of these concerns the state. Both the classical and the neoclassicism model conceive the modern state as sovereign in respect of security and justice. Whatever the differences that existed between the 'governmental project' to enhance the efficient and equitable administration of justice (clearly implicit in Beccaria's demand for a calculus of punishment) and the 'Lombrosan project' to differentiate criminals from non-criminals by the application of positivist means (Garland, 1997), each regarded the state in this way, a view which had considerable implications for the future of criminal justice.

> Over time it [the state-centred system of criminal justice] has come to be administered by professional bureaucracies, utilising institutions, laws, and sanctions specially designed for that purpose. The historical processes of differentiation, statisation, bureaucratisation, and professionalisation are the key characteristics of what we might term the 'modernisation' of crime control and criminal justice.
>
> (Garland, 2001: 30)

The second area of continuity is in respect of physical coercion. However much the demands of the classical punishment mentality (such as the principle of applying physical punishment to rational-culpable offenders) might have been mollified by the influences of neoclassicism (through the principle of mitigation) the coercive basis of the punishment model has, inevitably, placed limits on the practices which may co-exist with it. This much is borne out by recent experience. From the 1970s there was increasing scepticism about the therapeutic–rehabilitative model on the grounds that it was both ineffective and invasive. As a result, there was a growing demand, first in North America (American Friends Service Committee, 1971) and later in Europe, for a reversion to 'just deserts' principles. Support for an approach that emphasises just deserts (sometimes called the justice model) came from a rag-bag of groups: lawyers wishing to restore due process in order to confront the injustice of indeterminate sentences; radicals who saw proportionality as a means of reducing imprisonment for petty offences committed by the working class; radicals who believed that the elimination of judicial discretion would reduce prejudicial sentencing against blacks; and, last but not least, a radical right 'law and order' lobby which wanted to sweep aside the rehabilitative ideal and replace it with harsher and more retributive regimes. Though the demand for just deserts enabled liberals to express their legitimate concerns about disproportionate sentencing, more than anything else (and much to the chagrin of its authors) it legitimised right-wing demands for retribution to be exerted in the justice system. The result was a shift to harshly punitive justice policies in North America and to a lesser, though significant, degree in the UK. The example demonstrates that whatever liberal potential may be contained within the just deserts model, its coercive basis resonates with a visceral quality which tends to legitimise punitive retribution. In the following section we explore that visceral quality further by considering coercive force as a technology of governance.

## Force as a technology of governance

Force may be used as a technology of governance in a number of different ways and for a number of different ends. Here we discuss three different cases of the application of coercive force. Probably the most rudimentary use of physical force occurs when retributive punishment is enacted. Here, the aim is to 'govern the past' by employing physical force in order to 'right a wrong'. Consider the following example from the great southern African storyteller, Doris Lessing (1991: 9–10).

> There was once a highly respected and prosperous farmer . . . in the old Southern Rhodesia, now Zimbabwe, where [Lessing] grew up. . . . The farmer . . . decided to import a very special bull from Scotland. . . . He cost £10,000. . . . [I]t was a very large sum for the farmer. . . . A special home was made for him. . . . He had his own keeper, a black boy of about twelve. All went well; it was clear the bull would soon become the father of a satisfactory number of calves. . . . Then he suddenly and quite inexplicably killed his keeper, the black boy.

Something like a court of justice was held. The boy's relatives demanded, and got, compensation. But that was not the end of it. The farmer decided that the bull must be killed. When this became known, a great many people went to him and pleaded for the magnificent beast's life. After all, it was in the nature of bulls to suddenly go berserk, everyone knew that. The herd boy had been warned, and he must have been careless. Obviously, it would never happen again . . . to waste all that power, potential, and not to mention money – what for?

'The bull has killed, the bull is a murderer, and he must be punished. An eye for an eye, a tooth for a tooth,' said the inexorable farmer, and the bull was duly executed by firing squad and buried.

[In commenting on this series of events, Lessing notes, that] what [the farmer] had done – this act of condemning an animal to death for wrong-doing – went back into the far past of mankind, so far back we don't know where it began, but certainly it was when man hardly knew how to differentiate between humans and beasts.

[Lessing goes on to note how] tactful suggestions [not to execute the bull] from friends or from other farmers were simply dismissed with: 'I know how to tell right from wrong, thank you very much.'[2]

Lessing's story illustrates the visceral quality that can be evoked by coercive technologies when they are used to 'govern the past'. Sometimes, however, that quality may be obscured by other components of the governance process. This is illustrated in our second example that concerns the application of capital punishment as a deterrent technology for purposes of 'governing the future'. By the end of 1999, the death penalty was authorised in thirty-eight US states and by the Federal Government. Methods of execution currently in use include electrocution (used by eleven states), the gas chamber (used by five), hanging (used by three), the firing squad (used by three) and lethal injection (used by thirty-four and by the US military and the US government).

Timothy McVeigh, the Oklahoma City bomber was executed on 16 May 2001 by lethal injection. During this process, the condemned person is secured with lined ankle and wrist constraints on a gurney (a table or trolley). Cardiac monitor leads and a stethoscope are then attached and two saline intravenous lines are started, one in each arm. Next, the condemned person is covered with a sheet, the saline lines are turned off, and the individual constituents of the lethal injection are administered sequentially (*Agitator*, 2001). Lethal injection consists of sodium thiopental (which sedates the person), pancuronium bromide (a muscle relaxant which collapses the diaphragm and lungs) and potassium chloride (which stops the heart). The offender is usually pronounced dead within approximately seven minutes of the administration of the injection. The cost of drugs per execution in Texas is put at $86.08 (Texas Department of Criminal Justice, 2001).

Prison officials involved in McVeigh's execution were required to apply the Federal Bureau of Prisons 'Execution Protocol', a detailed manual specifying the exact procedures to be undertaken during the execution process. The Protocol, a fifty-four-page document, addresses everything from the purchase of the chemicals which killed McVeigh to the final clean-up of the site after the execution was completed. Among other things, the manual gives detailed instructions about the pre-execution procedures which must be carried out (including the systematic logging of all execution activities at the precise times at which they occur); the sequence of events to take place during the thirty minutes prior to the execution (including the removal of the condemned person from the holding cell, the strip-searching and dressing of the individual in designated clothing, the procedure for restraining the condemned person to the execution table and the admission of witnesses); the countdown to the execution (including the condemned individual's right to utter any 'reasonably brief' last words, the transcription of those words by Board of Prison staff for distribution to the media, and the Warden's declaration to begin the execution with the words 'We are ready'); the administration of the lethal injection; the determination of time of death; the removal of the body; the clean-up of the execution facility by staff trained in infectious disease preventive practice; and the final return of the prison facility to routine operations.

This example illustrates a paradox between two aspects of capital punishment: the deterrent effect that is claimed for it; and its routinised administration by specialist criminal justice agents. Far from being a calibrated mode of governance, execution is an unlimited one. (Beccaria's opposition to the death penalty arose, precisely, from the fact that it lay outside any rational calculus of punishment.) The rationale for execution as a deterrent technology of governance is, then, simple: deterrence (for the individual and for others) resides in the certainty of its severity. Readers familiar with

Foucault's (1977) account of the brutal execution of Damien in 1757 will be familiar with this idea. (The body, after being subjected to red-hot pincers, molten lead, boiling oil, burning resin, hot wax and sulphur, was drawn and quartered by six horses, before being reduced to ashes.) But the reader will also be struck by how far the Protocol is devoid of such visceral components and their intended general deterrent effects. What is most striking about the document is its 'proceduralisation' of governance. In other words, capital punishment, far from being enacted as a symbolic deterrent, is merely applied as a neutral technology for terminating life, not unlike the smart bombs of the Gulf War. It is administered by assigned professional officials; regulated by instructions having a high degree of specificity; implemented according to a precisely defined timetable; normalised through a process of closure which re-establishes the institutional status quo; and, above all else neutralised, by virtue of its application as an instrumental technology. The contrast between this deterrent version of capital punishment and the retributive one described by Lessing is, therefore, considerable. In Lessing's example visible pain is inflicted in order, symbolically, to 'right a wrong' through the application of force. In the present example, neither the symbolism nor the visibility of force is at issue. On the contrary, force is sanitised and obscured by the application of instrumental-technical rules. Whatever symbolic elements exist – and the visceral nature of much of the support for the death penalty within the US suggests they do – they are carefully masked so as to foreground a civilised sensibility in a process that resonates with CNN's construction of the events of the Gulf War.

Let us explore this issue of instrumentality in a third example which, like the first, also relates to an animal. On this occasion the incident involved the castration of a colt on a farm, witnessed by one of us while waiting to start a horse ride in the mountains near Cape Town. Before the castration began a woman came up and introduced herself as the owner of the farm. She said that something rather ugly was about to take place, but that it had to be done and that the persons doing it were very competent. The colt, she insisted, would be healed within a few days and there would be no infection. At that point the castration process began. First a nose twitch was put on the colt. (The nose twitch is a rope attached to the end of the animal's upper lip. Since this is a tender part of the animal's body, tightening of the apparatuses causes pain and thus facilitates control.) Being spirited, the colt fought the twitch and the people holding it. The stallion of the herd, excited and worried by the events, repeatedly approached the colt but was waved away. Soon, the men working on the colt attached ropes to its body in a pulley-like arrangement with one of the ends fastened to the animal's hind legs. Once the mechanism was in place the men tightened the ropes and the colt went down. The force that the ropes had been designed to apply worked well, and the colt was soon subdued. Once this happened the half a dozen men held the animal down with their combined strength and the castration began. The scrotum was disinfected, the testicles were quickly cut off and medication to encourage healing was applied. Then the ropes were removed. With the nose twitch still in place, the colt was led off with soothing words into a small corral containing mares. Then the next colt, older and quieter than the previous one, was roped and the procedure was repeated.

Throughout this process the men were competent and efficient, going about their work professionally. Indeed, such was their level of expertise that they were able to talk and joke with each other as they applied the various techniques, each participant knowing his role and playing it well. Force was only applied for a specific purpose, never gratuitously. In effect, coercion and pain were deployed efficiently in order to institute a programme of governance, the object of which was to ensure that only designated stallions could impregnate mares. The roping techniques used, formed part of the broader technology for governing horses in order that they should remain suitable for human purposes.

This incident illustrates the traditional Hobbesian[3] approach to governing through force exemplified in the classical Beccarian model of punishment. The aim of this mentality of governance – which Foucault describes as 'rule' – is to gain the compliance of the governed subject so that the ends of the ruler are realised. In Foucault's view a paradigmatic example of that approach may be found in Machiavelli's book, *The Prince*, a volume of instruction on practices of rule. According to this approach, physical coercion is the principal technology for achieving compliance and effecting rule. As was demonstrated in our discussion of classical punishment, coercive technologies involve two related aspects. First, they apply pain to the body in order to change the will and, by so doing, encourage the subject (human or animal) to act in ways that comply with the ruler's objectives. Second, they constrain bodies so that they are unable to be deployed as instruments of the will, and by so doing, prevent them from acting in ways which contravene the ruler's objectives.

The colt story illustrates both of these forms of coercive technology and also reflects aspects of the 'punitive style of control' described by Cohen (1994). The nose twitch was designed to inflict pain – as and when necessary – in order to shape the colt's will and enforce its compliance; the ropes acted to constrain the animal's movements; the team of men enacted a programme of rule with calculated (instrumental) efficiency; as professionals they constituted specialists delegated to operate on behalf of a higher authority, the farm owner; the overall aim of that programme was to 'govern the future' so that the colt would no longer have the capacity to impregnate mares.

During this procedure the colt also received its first serious lesson in the ruling mentality of humans, an experience that will undoubtedly be repeated many times over. As the newly formed gelding grows up, it will be shaped and constrained in very similar ways to ensure that it complies with the will of the people – the riders and trainers – who will rule it. When this happens, the nose twitch will be replaced by bits and spurs and the rope constraints with halters and stables – tools which, through the application of necessary and calibrated force, will ensure that its will is compliant.

This attitude towards governance is reflected in the criminal justice system. For example, one finds it in police programmes for the graduated escalation of force (Table 1). What we are suggesting is that state police officers are comparable to the team of castrators described in our story. As professionals, they apply force and, by so doing, try to shape wills and constrain bodies in the furtherance of ruling objectives. To be 'professional' in this context means to work effectively and efficiently within the framework of proportionality. They will seek first to persuade (to police by consent) and, if this fails, will employ an escalating level of force in order to achieve

*Table 1* Escalating levels of tactical objective and their action correlates

|   | Tactical objective | Activity/instrument |
|---|---|---|
| 1 | Persuade | Dialogue |
| 2 | Compliance | Escort |
| 3 | Compliance | Inflict pain |
| 4 | Compliance | Use of mechanical devices (stun grenades, etc.) |
| 5 | Impede | Use of baton, CS gas, TASER, etc. |
| 6 | Stop | Use of firearm |

*Source:* McKenzie, 2000: 182. Adapted from Parsons, 1980.

compliance. As professionals, they take no pleasure in this, and will seek to apply the minimum degree of force whenever it is possible to do so.

Despite sustained criticism about its moral appropriateness and instrumental effectiveness this approach to governance has proved remarkably resilient. For that reason it continues to have a major impact on state institutions, on the agents employed by them and on the cultures that underpin them. As we suggested earlier, one explanation for this resilience is the elegance of the punishment mentality, a single act being applied both to the governance of the past and to the governance of the future. Punishment is used to right past wrongs through retribution. Then it is used to reduce future harms through deterrence, sometimes – as was demonstrated in the colt story – with the added bonus of incapacitation.

According to this mentality, institutions of governance are imbued with a knowledge of force and equipped with a capacity to deploy it. Bittner recognises this in his classic definition of a state police: 'a mechanism for the distribution of non-negotiably coercive force employed in accordance with the dictates of an intuitive grasp of situational exigencies' (1991: 48). By functioning to maintain order through the application of non-negotiable force, the police institution makes actionable the mentality and technology of the Hobbesian paradigm of rule.

In later chapters we show that there are alternative ways of governing security which operate outside this Hobbesian frame-work and which require the mobilisation and coordination of different capacities and associated knowledges. To close this chapter let us simply indicate the general principle at stake by returning, briefly, to our equestrian example. The traditional coercive paradigm for dealing with horses is simple: '1. Just saddle a horse and get on. 2. Kick him to go. 3. Pull the reins to stop' (Parelli, 1993: iv). Contrast this with the mentality and technology being promoted by 'horse-whisperers', a term taken from a book and movie that celebrated an alternative approach to governing horses. This approach requires a multi-capacity technology and gives rise to different practices from those produced by the conventional model. Thus, while many 'traditional' tools (bits, halters, spurs and so on) are employed under the alternative mentality, they perform different functions from before and are, therefore, accorded new meanings.

## Notes

1 More sophisticated theorists argue that the reason for adopting a backward-looking logic is rational and moral rather than emotive. They argue that a retributive logic ensures that burdens imposed on people are justified in terms of their actions rather than on the grounds that punishing them will be good for others.

2 We would like to thank Rich Jones for bringing this story to our attention.

3 Thomas Hobbes was a seventeenth-century English political philosopher.

# 4

# HISTORICAL SHIFTS IN SECURITY GOVERNANCE

## Introduction

In Chapter 3 we focused attention on the mentality that underlies the punishment paradigm. This mentality defines punishment as the necessary and obvious tool to be used in governing security. According to its logic, governmental ends can only be achieved through the exercise of pain and constraint, all alternative possibilities being literally 'unthinkable'. We saw this mentality in action when the stud owner insisted that though something ugly was about to happen, it was both necessary and unavoidable if the stud's objectives were to be met. However, this 'taken for granted' assumption about the inevitability of punishment is not only the product of a particular mentality. That mentality is, itself, embedded in practices which become habitual. These, in turn, 'contain' the technology, the organisation and the mentality of governance which is being deployed. To suggest this, is not to claim that practices are 'determined'; nor is it to deny that those who deploy them may reflect upon what they have done in order to improve their procedures and transmit their techniques more effectively. Rather, as Foucault suggests, thought is less a 'cause' of action than part of a process in which practice and reflection work together. Through 'imagination' or 'problematisation' (Foucault, 1988) thought produces images of practice which, in turn, reflect back on that practice. While no practice is thoughtless, neither thought nor practice are reducible to one another. The relationship between mentalities, practices, institutions and technologies is enabling rather than determining.

This point is central to the discussion which follows. In this chapter we focus on the 'front-end' of security governance: that is to say, on the modern police institution and on the policing arrangements which preceded it. Our contention is that while the institutions and technologies of policing have changed considerably over the centuries, they remain linked to an underlying mentality of punishment whose influence, though challenged, continues to be significant. The chapter is organised into three sections. In the first we distinguish the 'governance-based' approach adopted here from the 'interest-based' one which dominates the Anglo-American model of police history. The second section examines the historical shift from community-based/distanciated forms of security governance to professional/state-centred forms. In the final section we consider the more recent shift from punishment-centred to problem-oriented modes of security governance.

## The limits of the Anglo-American model of police history

Though this chapter is about historical change within the police it is important to distinguish our approach from that found in mainstream histories of the growth and consolidation of the 'new police' in Britain and North America. The dominant Anglo-American model of policing regards the emergence of public police forces in the nineteenth century as a state-led response to the crime and disorder problems associated with capitalist industrialisation and urbanisation. The Anglo-American model contains two diametrically opposed versions of how and why this process occurred, the first a conservative (or 'orthodox') explanation, the second a radical (or 'revisionist') one.

The orthodox account of the emergence of the new police in Britain (Reith, 1952; Critchley, 1978; Ascoli, 1979) is a relatively straightforward one. Rapid industrialisation and urbanisation, it is suggested, gave rise to escalating levels of crime and disorder which the existing system of policing – old, disorganised, ineffective, inefficient and corrupt – was simply incapable of dealing with. At that point, the creativity and foresight of certain political leaders, notably Peel, initiated a state-led solution to the problem, though one that, crucially, remained sympathetic to the protection of individual liberty. Peel's new police, it is argued, achieved high standards of efficiency, effectiveness, and integrity without the degree of centralisation that would have threatened personal freedoms. For orthodoxy, the 'police solution' was, thus, not merely a product of historical need but also a reflection of the culture of 'Englishness': as Reiner puts it: '[t]he irresistible force of industrialisation and its control problems, meeting the immovable object of stubborn English commitment to liberty, could result in only one outcome: the British bobby (2000: 23).

The revisionist position (e.g. Storch, 1975, 1976; Spitzer and Scull, 1977) traces the need for police reform less to simple fear of crime and disorder than to the capitalist state's need to pacify and discipline an unpredictable industrial working class. For revisionists, the alienating effects of capitalism produced social tensions that, from the state's point of view, demanded disciplinary solutions. However, the existing system of parish constables, whose class allegiances might be suspect, could not be trusted to effect such discipline. Nor was it possible to rely upon the patchwork system of commercial and communal protection that existed, unevenly, throughout the country. The obvious solution was, therefore, to establish a trained professional public police force that could be relied upon to carry out the state's requirements. This solution was, itself, part of a much wider political project whereby the costs of reproduction of labour power would gradually be socialised through the collective provision of health, welfare and protection. As Reiner, again, puts it: '[i]ntermittent and spasmodic law enforcement dependent upon private initiative was replaced by continuous state policing financed by the public purse' (2000: 29–30). For the revisionist, then, the new police were concerned not merely with crime control and prevention, but with the widest possible imposition of discipline on working class people. Thus, Storch (1976) maintains, the new police not only undertook crime control and order maintenance duties, they also acted as 'domestic missionaries', subjecting the leisure pursuits of the working class to levels of discipline equivalent to those which they experienced when working in the factories.

Despite the ideological differences between orthodoxy and revisionism, the Anglo-American model, as a whole, may be criticised on a number of grounds. First, both orthodox and revisionist historians fall foul of the rationalistic conception of action (Hindess, 1982): the fallacious view that policy outcomes are the product of rational decision making on the part of agents.

> Both the traditional and revisionist views of police history portray the development of the police in terms of rational solutions to genuine problems. In the traditional view it is great, far-sighted men who recognise the solutions; in the radical alternative the solutions tend to be class needs.
>
> (Emsley, 1996: 5)

Now, it is all very well to claim that agents – whether enlightened politicians or capitalist states – have reasons for acting in the ways that they do, but it is quite a different matter to contend that policy outcomes are the product of such rational decision-making processes. Consider, for example, the many problematic assumptions which lie behind the claim that the Victorian state established the new police either in order to control crime and disorder or to secure the interests of developing capitalism: that the constituent elements of the state possessed common objective interests; that they had a means of recognising and a willingness to act upon those interests; that they possessed the necessary capacities to carry out such action, including the knowledge to decide that one action was more 'rational' than any other; and that by undertaking such actions, they could guarantee achieving their objectives by eradicating or circumventing the effects of inauspicious or unsympathetic social and political conditions. Every one of these assumptions is highly dubious. The emergence of the new police cannot be accounted for in rationalist terms.

Second, both orthodox and revisionist versions of police history operate with teleological and functionalist conceptions of change. For example, Reiner's (2000) depiction of the orthodox account of the emergence of the British 'bobby' which we referred to earlier, describes a mixture of functionalism and evolutionism – backed up by a good measure of cultural determinism – whose product ('the police solution') is contained within a teleological model of change. Though substantively different, the revisionist account – in which the 'police solution' arose as a functional corollary of the structural demands of capitalism – operates with similar theoretical assumptions. Such explanation gives rise to serious problems. For example, it is clear that local studies of police history show a degree of variation in patterns of development that the Anglo-American model is unable to explain (see Johnston, 1992b: chapter 10).

Third, the Anglo-American model is predicated upon what might be termed an 'interest-based' explanation of practices and outcomes. For revisionists, police reform is a product of the ruling class's capacity to secure its class interests over and above the class interests of the proletariat. For orthodoxy the 'police solution' is implemented successfully because the new police are said to encapsulate the interests of the wider community and, by so doing, are able to win widespread public legitimacy. There are two problems with such interest-based explanations. On the one hand, the argument that people's 'interests' (we prefer to use terms such as

59

'objectives' or 'concerns' and do so throughout this book) reside in economic class relations (revisionism) or in wider social relations (orthodoxy) is unconvincing. On the contrary, people's concerns and objectives are situated, constructed and re-constructed within complex and dynamic processes rather than merely 'given' by the 'nature of things' (Johnston, 1986). On the other hand, the effect of such interest-based explanation is to simplify a complex reality, the effects of which are similar to the effects of teleology. In effect, interest-based explanations reduce policing to a mere epiphenomenon, failing to recognise it as a determinate set of institutions and practices whose specific character will vary from time to time and from place to place.

This interest-based conception is important for two reasons. First, it underpins – and to a significant degree makes possible – the rationalistic and teleological assumptions criticised previously. Second, it supports an essentialist view of policing. That is to say, it endows police with the fulfilment of certain essential functions (see Wright, 2002 for an interesting critique of this tendency). In contrast to this interest-based view of policing, we propose a governance-based one. This approach makes no 'essentialist' assumptions about *inter alia* the functions of the police, the ends which they serve, the objectives which they pursue, the means by which they pursue them or the historical trajectory through which police institutions develop. Thus, although we argue that the punishment mentality has had a crucial impact on the institutions, practices and technologies of policing during the last two centuries, we do not consider that mentality to constitute the essence of policing. On the contrary, we argue that a full understanding of historical shifts in security governance demands an exploration of the interface between contrasting mentalities and their related institutions, technologies and practices.

## From distanciated to state-centred security governance

The institutions and the technologies through which 'front-end' security practices are applied have changed drastically over the centuries. However, the underlying basis of their mentality – the application of force as both a source of pain and a means of constraint – has remained relatively constant. Prior to the consolidation of the modern European state, the foundation of rule lay in kinship structures and local community networks. These institutions obliged citizens to watch for persons who violated order so that they might be apprehended and punished. Governing authorities – kings and later state governments – obliged citizens to perform designated tasks on their behalf, thereby effecting governance through collective-communal means. Such tasks were directed at both governing the past and governing the future. For instance, citizen patrols would be required both to expel suspicious strangers and to bring forward for punishment person's who had violated the sovereign's order. These institutions and technologies sought to facilitate 'rule at a distance' (Rose, 1996) on the part of governing authorities rather than requiring them to secure direct control over subjects. Punishment, in this arrangement, was used both as a tool for responding to wrongdoers and as a means of persuading citizens to fulfil their responsibilities in effecting governance at a distance.

Many of these features were apparent in England. The Anglo-Saxon system was communally structured, with tythingmen (responsible for the good conduct of groups of ten families or tythings) reporting upwards to hundredmen (responsible for groups of one hundred families) who, in turn, reported to shire reeves or sheriffs (the shire being a unit of about 120 hundreds). The sheriff bore responsibility for the preservation of the King's Peace in the shire and it was his responsibility, when an emergency arose, to muster the 'hue and cry' (or *posse comitatus*). All members of the community were under obligation to participate in the hue and cry, and refusal could result in punishment. Punishment was also implicit in the pursuit of felons. For example, legislation passed during the tenth century placed responsibility on the hundreds to report suspicious movements of cattle and to flog thieves when caught. More generally, when offenders were apprehended, stolen property would be returned to victims, while the offender's property could be seized and divided up between the hundred and the lord (Robinson *et al.*, 1994). After the Norman Conquest of 1066 the system was subjected to greater centralisation. It was also during this period that the title of constable (a Norman term) was first employed. Emsley (1996) notes that by the middle of the thirteenth century the name covered a variety of functionaries including the high constables of the hundreds and the petty constables (eventually to be known as parish constables) of the manors, tythings or vills. The latter officials, whose authority derived from the communal traditions of the Anglo-Saxon period, as well as bearing responsibility for the King's Peace, were also required to make reports to the local courts leet (manorial courts) about felons, miscreants and nuisances.

In addition to that, the office of watchman was formalised in the Statute of Winchester 1285. Under the terms of that legislation all boroughs were required to provide watches of twelve men organised on a rota basis, while smaller towns had to find between four and six watchmen depending upon the size of their populations. A separate act 'divided the City of London into twenty-four wards, each of which was required to have a watch of six men supervised by an alderman, while a "marching watch" was to "patrol the whole city"' (Emsley, 1996: 9). In all cases, the watch was to be stationed at the town gate between sunset and sunrise with watchmen having powers to arrest strangers during hours of darkness. All able-bodied men were required to undertake regular service in the watch and refusal to do so could lead to a spell in the stocks. The Statute of Winchester preserved and codified two features from earlier days. Though Critchley (1978) suggests that the Statute initiated watch and ward, it is clear that it built upon an already functioning system dating back to Roman and Anglo-Saxon times. This was hardly surprising since 'it is difficult to imagine any group of people, sufficiently organised and concerned to construct a wall around their community, who would not take the obvious next step and defend it' (Griffiths, 2000: 19). The second feature was the institutionalisation of hue and cry, all members of the local community being required to lay aside work in the pursuit of fugitives. Failure to do this was to be regarded as equivalent to favouring the felon and would, in turn, justify sanctions.

A central feature of these arrangements was a mechanism that permitted governing agents to observe what was taking place within their localities. The surveillance upon which these arrangements depended did not require specialist intelligence gathering skills. On the contrary, the knowledge required was an unexceptional feature of everyday life linked to the transparency of collective life within small, close-knit rural communities. (Later we shall see that transparency remains an essential feature of contemporary regimes of distanciated governance.) These institutional arrangements changed in two ways as kingdoms gave way to nation states. First, the governance of security was brought, more and more, under state auspices. Second, the business of governance moved increasingly from lay to specialist hands. These developments were not, of course, peculiar to 'front-end' criminal justice institutions. A parallel development was occurring at the 'back-end' of security governance with the emergence of the prison as a specialised means for the application of calibrated pain. It was, however, at the 'front-end' of security governance that the impact of these developments was revealed most clearly.

Two factors were especially important in shaping these developments. First, in urban centres, like London, the transparency requirements upon which strategies of governance at a distance depended were being undermined. During the sixteenth and seventeenth centuries London was faced with a growing and mobile population, an expanding crime problem and the emergence of a number of unregulated areas. Some of these areas harboured law-breakers under feudal rights of sanctuary which, though having been legally terminated more than a century before, persisted in a residual form. Enforcement agents found it difficult to penetrate these areas and, as a result, the central state employed a variety of means (including patronage, nepotism and commercial initiatives) to facilitate effective surveillance. Under these conditions effective rule at a distance was increasingly difficult to achieve; or, as McMullan puts it, 'formal state control was an elaborate, negotiated and tenuous artifice [based upon] a fluid system of patron-client power blocs' (1987: 123). McMullan's point is a critical one since it reminds us that governance at a distance, far from being the inevitable product of the governing agent's will, is a strategy whose realisation, or lack of realisation, is conditioned by a variety of factors.

Second, distanciated strategies of rule based upon the deployment of private agents, such as informants and thief-takers, posed problems – but also released potentials – of their own. Thief-takers, such as Jonathan Wilde, demanded that victims make payment for the return of their stolen goods, a system that was by no means peculiar to England. (In eighteenth-century Massachusetts, the procedure was called 'theft-bote'.) The problem was, of course, that such private resolutions were not only arbitrary and capricious – thief-takers often received rewards for the return of items that they had stolen themselves – they were also a challenge to state-imposed order. Thus, the rural aristocracy resisted the emergence of a state justice system precisely because it usurped their traditional capacity to control the exercise of local justice by informal means. Yet, the impact of private justice was by no means uniformly regressive. One of its effects was to shift the steering of governance to customers who, thus, became governing authorities themselves. In Philadelphia private prosecution was widely used until the formation of a public police in 1854. People entered litigation for many different reasons: to gain justice; to extort money; to prevent prosecution against themselves; to intimidate others; and so on. Yet, the system gave people the 'freedom to police themselves' (Steinberg, 1986: 243) thereby ensuring a degree of popular control over justice. Predictably, legislators tried to dispense with a system that maximised consumer power and even after the formation of the public police, tension continued to arise between citizens and the state. For example, many of those arrested and prosecuted by the newly formed police continued to resist state monopolisation of justice by 'prosecuting policemen themselves, establishing informal methods of adjudication with magistrates, and simply fighting back' (ibid.: 244).

The new police reforms aimed, therefore, to address two perceived governmental problems: to replace 'rule at a distance' mechanisms that were perceived (by governmental programmers) to be working inadequately, not least in urban areas; and to respond to private initiatives in policing and prosecution which gave rise to arbitrary and capricious outcomes and which, by empowering consumers, constituted a direct obstacle to state steering. This last point is crucial. The main problem with private initiatives, from the perspective of state agents, was not that they were private but that they challenged developing state agendas. (Later we shall suggest that contemporary private security has flourished because it has neither been subjected to state steering nor has challenged state agendas.)

The new police reforms were driven by a preventive mentality. In part this was a reaction to the excesses of thief-takers who, while 'fighting crime', had also retained a stake in its continued existence. Having an organisation whose preventive goals would be implemented by salaried personnel rewarded from the public purse was, therefore, intended to eradicate the worst excesses of the old system. Interestingly, however, it was the old system that provided much of the inspiration for the new one. Colquhoun's *Treatise on the Police of the Metropolis* was the first work written about police in the English language and though Peel chose not to acknowledge any intellectual debt to Colquhoun (Bowden, 1978), the latter's Marine Police Establishment, founded in 1798, was a model police organisation. The force consisted of sixty armed men and cost £5,000 in its first year of operation, four-fifths of which was funded by the West India Company. Colquhoun's Marine Police consisted of paid employees whose function was to establish a programme of surveillance, making it more difficult for workers to remove property from the docks without apprehension. During the first year of its operation the force saved £100,000 worth of cargo (Clayton, 1967).

The principles upon which the Marine Police operated were characteristically Beccarian. By establishing an 'unremitting watch' over the docks and increasing the chances of apprehension and the certainty of punishment, it was assumed that people would be deterred from future wrongdoing. This idea was attractive to Peel and his advisors who reasoned that if such a strategy could work for the docks, it might also work for the city as a whole. This reasoning also fitted with the wider Peelian agenda of police reform. That agenda had several interrelated components: the desire to establish a salaried and professional preventive police force; the wish to have that organisation under state control; and the insistence that, state control notwithstanding, the new police would retain a civil status distinguishing them from the militarised police forces of certain continental regimes. The mechanism developed for facilitating this preventive project was the beat system, the idea being that the patrolling officer would both observe what was happening around him and would establish links with the local community, whose members would become the 'eyes and ears' of the police. In accordance with rational Beccarian principles, beats were carefully planned and measured, with specific obligations being placed on officers for patrolling them.

> In the Metropolitan Police district in the second half of the nineteenth century the average day beat was two miles. These had to be walked at a steady rate of two and a half miles an hour. During the day the constable patrolled on the kerbside of the pavement, at night he walked on the inner side from where he could more easily check bolts and fastenings.
>
> (Emsley, 1996: 225)

Two things may be noted about these developments. First, the new system combined direct surveillance by the police (through the beat system) with indirect surveillance by the public (who, it was hoped, would report crime and pass on information to the police). Each of these activities was intended to enhance citizen support for the new police. This idea of citizen support was, however, different from the previous system of direct citizen responsibility for policing. The new arrangements shifted that responsibility to professional police officers who relied on citizens to provide them with the means of fulfilling their duties. In Foucaultian terms, it might be said the state was being 'governmentalised', that is, endowed with new and additional governing responsibilities. Second, the Peelian system sought to prevent crime through the exercise of an 'unremitting watch' by a professional police force, the effect of which would be to ensure certain detection and punishment for those who dared to offend. It is important, however, not to conceive this punishment-based preventive mentality in essentialist terms. At the beginning of this chapter we suggested that the relationship between mentalities, practices, institutions and technologies was 'enabling', rather than 'determining'. This relationship is well exemplified in the new police reforms. For while the punishment mentality drove those reforms in a preventive direction, other factors added layers of complexity to the reality of policing. One such factor was the political situation in Ireland. Emsley (1996) notes that while the prevention of crime was emphasised as the primary objective of the Metropolitan Police, its uniform, discipline and organisation indicated that Peel – who had been instrumental both in establishing the Irish Peace Preservation Force in 1814 and in the development of the Irish Constabulary Act of 1822 – imported into London many of the policing practices developed in Ireland to deal with civil disorder. In the following section we consider several other conditions that complicated the developmental trajectory of the punishment-prevention model of policing.

## The shift from punishment to problem-solving

As we have just said, the Peelian model was based upon the idea of using surveillance to ensure certain detection, thereby facilitating prevention. In fact, this model aspired to a state in which the efficacy of prevention would reduce crime to a level where the need for detection would eventually be reduced: in other words, a situation where there would be less and less crime, and fewer and fewer criminals to apprehend. Arguably, this view assumed that surveillance, rather than force, would become the primary means of governing security. In practice, the assemblage of surveillance-deterrence-punishment-prevention conformed with the Beccarian model of 'calibrated' policing described at the end of the previous chapter. First, police would aim to police by consent – through community-based surveillance regimes – and second, if that failed, they would employ escalating levels of force in order to achieve compliance.

In fact, Peel's aspiration to ensure prevention through the certainty of detection and punishment has remained unrealised during the two centuries since the inception of the new police. There are a number of reasons for this, some of which relate to shortcomings within policing, others to problems within the wider criminal justice system. For example, during most of the post-war period, steadily rising rates of crime have exposed the limits of the Peelian project. Added to that, as Table 2 shows, the public's willingness to report offences cannot be taken for granted; the police's capacity to detect offences is limited; and the court's ability to secure convictions is restricted.

Two particular obstacles were critical in stopping the police from realising the 'unremitting watch' demanded by the preventive model. The first was that direct surveillance opportunities were restricted by the institutions of privacy that limited routine police presence to public areas. As a Canadian police executive expressed it to one of us many years ago, the institutions of privacy left the police on the streets, while most of the activities they wanted to gain intelligence about were taking place behind closed doors and drawn curtains. The second obstacle to Peel's surveillance strategy concerned the motives of citizens prepared to pass information on to the police. Many of these people – notwithstanding the limits to crime reporting noted in Table 2 – were victims of crime and, as such, were motivated by a desire that the police would bring offenders before the courts for appropriate punishment. In effect, this meant that the procurement of intelligence from victims required the police to focus less and less on prevention, and

*Table 2* Attrition within criminal justice

|  | All offences (%)* |
| --- | --- |
| Offences committed | 100.0 |
| Offences reported | 45.2 |
| Offences recorded | 24.3 |
| Offences cleared up | 5.5 |
| Offences resulting in a caution or conviction | 3.0 |
| Offences resulting in a conviction | 2.2 |
| Offences resulting in a custodial sentence | 0.3 |

*Source:* Digest 4: *Information on the Criminal Justice System in England and Wales*, London: Home Office (1999).

*Note*
*Criminal damage, theft of a motor vehicle, theft from a motor vehicle (including attempt), bicycle theft, domestic burglary, wounding, robbery/theft from the person.

more and more, on 'bandit-catching'. In other words, prevention demanded intelligence, but the acquisition of intelligence pushed the police away from a preventive role, towards a reactive, bandit-catching one.

What we are suggesting is that while police organisation reflected the Peelian mentality, the technology of surveillance, which that mentality demanded, could not be realised within the existing conditions. Thus, the grid-based system for distributing officers across beats became a mechanism for enabling police to respond promptly to calls for assistance from victims, rather than a basis for 'unremitting watch'. Accordingly, the police's inability to fulfil their preventive goals forced them, more and more, to focus on bandit-catching and detection. Here, there is an historical irony. Private security companies were originally established to detect crime yet, during the twentieth century adopted 'a glacial drift from a detection to a protection speciality' (Morn, 1982: ix). By contrast, during the same period, public police forces concentrated more and more on detection (through reactive bandit-catching rather than preventive surveillance) abandoning key elements of the Peelian model.

Over the years the police have adopted a variety of means to try and resolve these contradictions. Take, for example, the problem of the state's limited right to intrude on citizens' privacy. Here, police have adopted two responses. The first has been to argue for the imposition of limits on the institutions of privacy so that direct surveillance might be engaged in more easily. In Anglo-American policing systems this approach has led to considerable debate regarding police powers. In England and Wales, concern about the increasingly invasive potential of electronic surveillance was evident in the controversy about proposals contained in the Police Bill of 1997. Opposition amendments in the House of Lords rejected the Bill's proposals to give chief constables a statutory authority to plant bugs in pursuit of the prevention and detection of serious crime, proposing instead a system where police chiefs would seek authorisation from a commissioner. Particular concern arose that the nebulous definition of 'serious crime' – which included activities 'by a large number of persons in pursuit of a common purpose' – combined with the technical capacities of the equipment concerned, would facilitate police deviance. An editorial in the *New Law Journal* put it thus: the police 'have shown many times that they have not behaved well enough to allow them this additional right' (cited in *Police Review*, 24 January 1997: 5).

A second method has been to invest, more and more, in technological surveillance. A particularly good example concerns the application of CCTV in public places, particularly in Britain. CCTV is an exemplar of 'actuarial' technology since, under it, aggregate populations, as well as individual offenders, are subject to the camera's gaze. Inevitably, this raises questions about rights to privacy. British television viewers and newspapers readers are now routinely exposed to images drawn from the CCTV footage of public and private authorities. Currently, for example, the ITV network is broadcasting *Oblivious*, 'a comedy game show in which [the presenter] swoops to surprise unsuspecting people who have been caught on camera, and reveals that they might have unwittingly won a cash prize' (*Radio Times*, 11–17 August 2001: 67). The problem is, of course, that unsuspecting people may be captured on film unwillingly, as well as unwittingly. Some years ago, CCTV pictures of a couple engaged in sexual intercourse in a shop doorway were broadcast and published widely throughout the national media. Of course, CCTV may be used for purposes other than entertainment. Both the previous Conservative government and the present Labour administration have invested massively in the technology for crime prevention purposes, despite little evidence being available as to its efficacy in this regard. Cameras are now found routinely throughout British towns and cities, and with recent legislation having been passed enabling police authorities to retain the fine income from motorists caught on speed cameras and use it for investment in road safety measures, such cameras are proliferating daily.

Inevitably, these developments raise controversy. In August 1996 Strathclyde Police decided to issue pictures obtained from a Glasgow red-light district, in order to aid an investigation into the murder of a prostitute. The decision was criticised on the grounds that it might damage the reputation of those caught on camera. However, the police argued that if witnesses did not come forward voluntarily, there was justification to release their photographs for publication. It is interesting to contrast these British examples with a recent Canadian judgement. Mr George Radwanski, the Federal Privacy Commissioner, enacting his first decision under the Personal Information Protection and Electronic Documents Act (PIPED), notified Centurion Security Services Co. Ltd that their installation of surveillance cameras at a street intersection in Yellowknife was unlawful. In his decision, Radwanski held that both live video pictures and recorded video pictures of individuals qualify as 'personal information' under the Act, and as such, cannot be collected or used in the context of a commercial activity without informed consent. Though he acknowledged that there may be instances where it is appropriate for public places to be monitored for public safety reasons, Radwanski ruled that such surveillance must be limited to instances where there is some demonstrable need, adding that 'people have a right to go about their business without feeling that their actions are being systematically observed and monitored. That is the very essence of the fundamental human right to privacy . . .' (Privacy Commissioner of the North West Territories, News Release, 20 June 2001).

Recently, police have adopted a somewhat different tack in attempting to achieve Peel's preventive objectives. In doing so, they have given new life to the Peelian strategy of citizen participation in policing by extending it beyond the mere provision of intelligence. According to this view, citizens, now conceived as fully-fledged partners of the police, are deemed to have a significant responsibility for security governance. Moreover, the concept of partnership that underpins this model extends not only to citizens but is also dispersed across the wider state and civil society. This way of making up the world as a terrain of governance aims, among other things, to de-specialise the governance of security. As a result, it is argued that non-specialised state agents (such as education, health and housing departments), commercial organisations, voluntary bodies and 'responsible citizens', have a collective duty to work alongside specialised police organisations in pursuit of security goals. The result is that the governance of security is no longer regarded as the exclusive responsibility of the 'public sector'. Rather, governance is linked to and contained within terrains that, historically, have been defined as non-governmental. The result is that the spheres of 'the governed' and 'the governing' are now less distinct than hitherto. (Or, as some writers prefer to express it, the public and the private spheres have become blurred.) Governance is now everybody's business.

Significantly, while re-invoking Peel's preventive dream, this shift ceases to regard deterrence as either the principle or the sole means for achieving it. In challenging deterrence it denies the Hobbesian and Beccarian view that governance must be rooted in pain/punishment. However, the challenge neither claims that pain can never be effective; nor that it should never be employed; nor that its imposition is inherently wrong. Rather, it conceives pain as one of a number of means that may be utilised to govern security. This re-conception of the use of pain challenges, fundamentally, the punishment paradigm which we outlined in Chapter 3 without, however, abandoning pain as a governmental resource. In effect the shift we describe is a highly specific one, for while a paradigm change has taken place the existing institutions and technologies of punishment have also been maintained. It is the specific character of this shift that explains why the established institutions for the application of force (police, courts and corrections) have tolerated and even supported the paradigm change. In effect, punishment has been incorporated as a governing resource within these broader changes.

The concept that lies at the core of these changes is 'problem-solving'. Problem-solving replaces Peel's central concept, surveillance, as the key to preventive governance. The idea underlying surveillance was that, by shaping the mental calculations guiding people's actions, a realisable promise of pain would be created, and with it, a preventive regime established. Though problem-solving is also predicated upon rational actors making calculations, these actions are not simply seen in terms of pain and its avoidance. Rather, people are seen to be engaged in complex calculations that take into account the multiple factors influencing behaviour, including the varied conditions constituting opportunities or obstacles to particular courses of action. The problem-solving approach conceives security governance differently from the punishment paradigm. A good illustration of the approach was described in Shearing and Stenning's (1987) account of policing in Disney World. Here a variety of devices were employed to solve people's problems in ways compatible with the Disney order, so that its governance would be achieved, primarily, through consensual rather than coercive means.

This shift in the mentality and technology of policing demands that we theorise security governance in a new way. Within the traditional paradigm policing was correctly defined by Bittner as the application of non-negotiable force by state officers having the legal right to do so. While this conception is perfectly compatible with the punishment paradigm it does not fit with the problem-solving model of governance. Within the latter paradigm the governance of security is identified as the application of any means that will promote safe and secure places in which people live and work. As neither the resources nor the modes of knowledge required to deploy them are monopolised by any set of persons or institutions, Peel's idea of public participation in policing is transformed from a situation in which people are mobilised as informants, to one in which they contribute their knowledge and capacities to problem-solving.

A simple illustration of this form of policing is given by Eck and Spelman (1987). Charlie Bedford complained to local police about rowdy teenagers keeping him awake with loud music and horseplay on Friday and Saturday nights. Sergeant Hogan, who received the call, assigned Officer Paul Summerfield to the problem. Summerfield suspected that the source of the disturbance was a roller skating rink which, in order to increase business, had recently reduced its prices and offered transportation to and from the venue on Fridays and Saturdays. Summerfield drove to the rink at two in the morning and found several large groups of youths hanging around. When questioned, they told him they were waiting for a bus. It transpired that, while the rink owner had leased a bus to pick up and drop off young people living at a distance from the rink, many others were left behind due to lack of places on the vehicle. The next evening Summerfield returned to the rink and noted that while fifty young people disembarked from the bus, many more arrived by public transport or were dropped off by a parent. Clearly, most of these would be stranded at the end of the evening. Officer Summerfield consulted with Sergeant Hogan and they agreed that the rink owner should be asked to bus all of the young people home. The owner agreed to this proposal and leased more buses. By the next weekend Summerfield and Hogan were able to confirm that no young people were disturbing Charlie Bedford's sleep. Sergeant Hogan summed it up as follows:

> Look, we can have the best of both worlds. People here can get their sleep and the kids can still have fun. But we can't do it by tying up officers and chasing kids every Friday and Saturday night. There has to be a way of getting rid of the problem once and for all.
>
> (Eck and Spelman, 1987: 50)

This example demonstrates the consensual dimension of problem-solving. People will participate in policing to the extent to which their involvement provides a 'win' for them as well as for the auspices seeking to govern security: in other words, a 'win–win' situation. Similar assumptions lie behind the 'broken windows' concept developed by Wilson and Kelling (1982). In this case, the idea is for community partners to undertake a variety of small actions (removing graffiti, picking up litter, etc.) in order to demonstrate that community order exists and is being maintained. We shall say more about this approach in Chapter 6.

## Concluding comments

The shift from punishment to problem-solving within security governance reflects Foucault's account of the movement from rule to government. Rule involves regulation from the outside. That is to say, the objective is to control a given terrain in order to secure the objectives of a ruler who sees himself/herself outside of the terrain being ruled. Government, by contrast, involves regulation from the inside. Here, the aim is to regulate life with the consent of the governed, organising things so that they contribute collectively to the regulatory regime. This mentality of governance – referred to by Foucault as 'the proper distribution of things' – captures nicely the problem-solving approach and its requirement to mobilise diverse capacities in the furtherance of order. The problem-solving approach also dovetails with the neo-liberal shift which has sought to promote responsible citizenship and which regards state-centred governance as ineffective and wasteful.

There are echoes in these developments of the period of 'distanciated rule' before Peel, though this is not to imply a return to the pre-Peelian era. The decentred forms of capacity and knowledge that exist today are embedded in organisational forms which differ substantially from those found in Peel's time. What is similar, however, is the desire to promote local capacity and knowledge as the basis for effective governance. It is for this reason that some contemporary writers have drawn attention to the 're-invention of government' (Osborne and Gaebler, 1993) and to the fact that governance is no longer monopolised by states. In Osborne and Gaebler's view, state governments can only continue to operate effectively if they shift from 'rowing' to 'steering'. While they are good at steering (because they are democratically elected to determine the direction of governance) they are poor at rowing (because they have neither the capacities nor the knowledge to carry out the directions of the electorate). Among other things, this approach implies a model of competition between the various agents (state, voluntary and commercial) in order to identify the best quality service providers.

Within security governance these developments have found their clearest expression in the movement within state police to embrace community policing. Community policing is an umbrella term describing a broad 'family' of initiatives through which police have sought to re-invent themselves and, by so doing, keep control of the steering of security governance while broadening the range of capacities, agents and knowledges engaged in its rowing. However, although community policing programmes share the broad family resemblance just described, they also vary significantly from one another. One critical dimension of variability concerns the extent to which programmes are willing to challenge the punishment paradigm and, by so doing, fully embrace the community model. At the least challenging end of the community policing continuum one finds programmes oriented towards mobilising citizens as informers so as to facilitate better bandit-catching. Such programmes take up neo-liberal ideas about the re-invention of government – not least in their desire to devolve rowing while continuing to monopolise steering – and continue to subscribe fully to the Peelian model of punishment. Not surprisingly such programmes have found much favour within traditional police organisations because of their desire to inject 'new wine into old bottles'. At the other end of the continuum, however, are problem-solving programmes, which by drawing upon neo-liberal ideas have seriously challenged the punishment paradigm. In the example described above, Officer Summerfield and Sergeant Hogan act both as bearers of force and as resource managers whose task is to analyse problems and assess needs. (In Britain some police forces have already designated beat officers as 'beat managers'.) It is not that problem-solving policing shifts the police entirely from the exercise of constraint and the application of pain. Rather, it places these resources within the context of other possible means. Prevention remains a critical feature of policing. What changes are the mentality, institutions, technology and practices for its accomplishment. To explore these developments further it is necessary to consider the contribution made by corporate auspices, something we address next in Chapter 5.

# 5

# CORPORATE INITIATIVES
## The risk paradigm

### Introduction

Having explored the institutions of the punishment paradigm we now reflect back on the challenges posed to that paradigm by the developments described in Chapter 1. In so doing we place our discussion of problem-solving from Chapter 4 into a broader context. Our discussion falls into three sections. The first explores the philosophy, technique and practice of risk management as it has developed in the sphere of corporate enterprise. The second section examines its impact outside the corporate sphere, first exploring some historical and legal aspects of risk-based practice, then considering its impact on civil society and the state with particular reference to security and justice. Among the examples considered here are the use of behavioural profiles in targetting offenders and offences, the role of risk management in the probation practice and the application of preemptive justice to those considered at high risk of offending. Drawing upon these developments, the third and final section examines further the relationship between the developing paradigm of risk and the traditional paradigm of punishment.

### Corporate risk management

It is now commonplace for criminologists to employ the language of risk when discussing criminality. Much work has been done on the impact of risk factors (prior conditions which increase the chances of an event's occurrence) on young people's criminal careers. Researchers, such as Farrington (1997) have undertaken extensive longitudinal studies in order to establish the ordering of factors in this regard. However, risk analysis is not only associated with offending behaviour. Increasingly, studies have attempted to identify features of people or things associated with patterns of victimisation, the results being used in the development of 'opportunity-reducing' crime prevention techniques (see Pease, 1997: 972 for an account of these – usually government sponsored – studies). Such research uses sophisticated techniques for the analysis of a wide range of offences, covering everything from murder to petty theft. However, it is important to recognise that risk is 'a way of thinking' (Douglas, 1992) before it becomes a set of deployable techniques. In order to illustrate the significance of this point, let us first explore risk-based thinking in its most 'natural' setting, the domain of the business corporation.

Risk-based thinking is fundamental to the corporate mentality, the efficacy of corporate capitalism being dependent, at least in part, on the deployment of rational economic calculation by managers. Such calculation is concerned with maximising corporate benefits in respect of things like product development, labour relations, business location or investment decisions. Correspondingly, it is also concerned with minimising any disbenefits which might arise from corporate activity. One way of doing this is to 'spread the risks' associated with business activity, insurance having become an important component in economic calculation from the early period of modern capitalism. From that early period companies employed risk managers to undertake certain specific tasks: to reduce, as far as possible, the company's need to purchase insurance; to optimise on the insurance expenditure it was required to make; and to minimise the company's exposure to both insurable and uninsurable risks (Bland, 1999).

In this context, risk may be defined as 'the calculable probability of occurrences that deleteriously affect the economic effectiveness of the company, whether financial, material or intangible (i.e. to reputation or legal status)' (ibid.: 13). This definition is a useful one since it emphasises that *any* calculable hazard – whether financial or non-financial, material or non-material, tangible or intangible – may constitute a potential obstacle to the economic security of the company. Accordingly, it is the job of corporate risk managers to anticipate, identify and appraise the seriousness of risks and to deploy actions to remove them. Where their removal is not possible, however, the risk manager will take steps to reduce the likely losses arising from them to a level considered 'acceptable' in the context of ongoing economic calculation (compare Broder, 1984).

Nalla and Newman (1990) provide a good account of how the philosophy of risk management is applied in practice, identifying a number of the elements which may be found in any corporate programme. First, it is necessary to review corporate policies, financial records and insurance files in order to determine which company assets may be at risk. Having examined corporate assets the risk manager then has to identify potential threats to those assets. Clearly these may have a variety of different sources ranging from 'acts of God' (such as fire and flood) to the vulnerabilities associated with particular locations (such as sales areas in retail premises or cash drawers in banks). More often than not, the most serious threats emanate from within the corporation. A survey undertaken by the Pinkerton Organization (1998) asked security managers to identify the top security threats facing corporate America. Out of twenty-three threats ranked by level of seriousness, the top six (employee theft, workplace violence, fraud and white collar crime, employee selection, hardware and software theft and unethical business conduct) involved employees within the workplace. The report concluded:

> While virtually every business today faces constant, serious external security issues, the most immediate threats are internal – in the workplace itself . . . The traditional 'fortress' mentality that emphasised protection against property crime, espionage, terrorism and threats to key personnel appears to be giving way to the realisation that internal matters can be more costly, and are certainly more prevalent.
>
> (Pinkerton Organization, 1998: 1)

Having identified assets and threats the security manager is then required to undertake risk assessment. This will involve assessing both the probability of adverse events occurring and the likely frequency of their re-occurrence. After that, it is necessary to estimate the probable losses arising from such occurrence. Though loss will be calculated in financial terms, such calculation is complex. For example, in the case of a bank robbery it is necessary to consider 'the recovery costs, replacement costs, loss of customer good-will, insurance costs, legal costs, business interruption, emotional health of employees, etc.' (Nalla and Newman, 1990: 94). Should a loss occur, the risk manager must next carry out an 'after-the-fact-assessment' so as to record the precise details of its occurrence (time, place, specific circumstances, etc.). By so doing, it is hoped to 'build up a picture of the choice structuring properties of the loss causing event' (ibid.: 95). This last comment is a particularly important one since it shows how the philosophy of risk-management assumes that perpetrators employ rational choice when carrying out criminal or other loss-inducing acts. We return to this point later.

The next stage in the process involves balancing any anticipated loss with the probability of its occurrence, a crucial factor in the rational deployment of security resources. Some occurrences (e.g. fires, earthquakes), though low in probability, generate high losses. Others (e.g. internal theft), though having high probability, generate small losses in unit terms but, as was demonstrated in the Pinkerton Organization (1998) study, give rise to large losses when aggregated. This means that important decisions have to be made both about the relative prioritisation of some risks over others and about the costs and benefits of engaging in different risk minimising strategies. Various control strategies may be employed in this regard (e.g. pre-employment screening of personnel, situational loss prevention techniques) but control is by no means the only form of minimisation. A company may decide to retain a given level of risk on the grounds that the benefits accruing to it outweigh any attendant disbenefits. Thus, businesses may choose to operate in locations where terrorism and kidnapping are rife precisely because profitability remains high. Nowadays contract security companies provide specialist services in this area. For example, Pinkerton's 'Global Intelligence Service' (GIS) functions to inform business executives about any international threats that might affect their interests or compromise the safety of their personnel. GIS staff are specialists in information analysis, criminal investigation, counter-intelligence, anti-terrorism, counterespionage and threat analysis, most of them having had extensive prior experience in military intelligence (Johnston, 2000b). Risk retention is, however, only one of several possibilities. Changes in business practice may enable losses to be displaced. Nalla and Newman (1990) cite the case of Automatic Teller Machines whose introduction may have reduced bank robberies at the price of increased customer muggings. Alternatively, security managers may be able to transfer those risks that are too costly or too difficult to accommodate to other agencies such as insurance companies.

Corporate risk management is oriented towards the prevention of loss. Two consequences follow from this orientation. First, corporate security focuses exclusively on governing the future, something that has distinguished it, in the past, from state security. Whereas security managers have one core objective to undertake, state police exercise dual roles. On the one hand, they are called upon to exercise (future-oriented) public *security* tasks, such functions being exemplified in phrases like 'the prevention of crime', 'the preservation of public tranquillity' and 'the maintenance of the Queen's Peace'. On the other hand, they are concerned with the administration of (past-oriented) criminal *justice* in respect of offenders and their victims. The exercise of justice is, after all, implicit in the demand that officers exercise their discretion 'judiciously', a defining feature of the office of constable.

Second, the primacy of loss prevention in risk management expands the population of those subjected to security. Again, comparison may be made with the actions of state police. In principle – if not always in practice – police direct their attention solely to those whom they have reason to suspect of having committed, or of being about to commit, an offence. By comparison, the security officer's gaze is wider. A good illustration is the use of 'snowflakes' described by one of us in an earlier study (Shearing and Stenning, 1981). This case concerned security officers who undertook evening site patrols on behalf of a major business corporation. Having identified security lapses, such as open windows and unlocked doors, officers would leave polite notes ('snowflakes') in the vicinity, outlining the nature of the problem. Duplicate copies of 'snowflakes' would be kept on file and management would interview habitual 'violators', once identified. This is a classic example of risk management in action, surveillance being directed not only at those responsible for the commission of offences but also at those who might, inadvertently, provide the opportunities for offences to take place. In the final section of this chapter we argue that the distinctions we have drawn between corporate agents and state police in respect of these two examples are now significantly less clear.

Programmes for risk minimisation in the 'proprietary' or 'in-house' security sector vary, but Cunningham and Taylor (1985) detect three broad components: physical security, information security and personnel security. Physical security is concerned with controlling and monitoring access, preventing unauthorised intrusion or surveillance, and safeguarding information, merchandise and buildings. Such security begins with perimeter protection (provided by barriers, fences, locks, CCTV, intrusion detection sensors, electronic alarms, security lighting, access control systems, guard stations, security patrols and the like). Similar means are used to minimise internal threat through the control of interior space. In some large organisations integrated security systems may be put into place, security functions (CCTV, access control, alarms) being linked to heating, ventilation and air conditioning systems with the integrated whole being monitored through a central station. Corporations also need to protect sensitive information such as product development plans, marketing plans, pricing information, customer mailing lists and documents relating to research and development. With developments in information technology, increased opportunity exists for theft of computer hardware and software, for misuse of computerised data and for interception of telecommunication transmissions. Moreover, with increased business reliance on the Internet, the risk of exposure to 'cyber crime' is also increased. Businesses may use in-house expertise to resolve these security problems or, more likely, will call upon the services of specialist consultants. Lastly, companies will take various steps to ensure the quality and integrity of their employees. Prospective employees may be screened as to their suitability for positions. In doing this, security managers may employ a variety of techniques: background investigation, credit checks, psychological tests, polygraph tests, criminal record checks and so on. Once suitable employees are in post, they may be required to participate in 'security awareness' programmes. Here the aim is to inculcate an appropriate security mentality in the new recruit: 'The ultimate goal . . . is to create a proprietary interest in the assets of the company so that they . . . feel a personal responsibility for prevention and reduction of losses' (Cunningham and Taylor, 1985: 44).

Cunningham and Taylor's distinction between the 'physical', 'intelligence' and 'personnel' elements of security provides a useful but rudimentary means of separating security functions within business organisations. We suggest that the following three-fold classification provides both greater conceptual precision and analytical scope. 'Opportunity management' refers to programme elements (personnel screening, profiling, the use of 'snowflakes', awareness programmes, etc.) directed towards the identification, construction, re-construction, mobilisation and reproduction of members who will comply with – and, ideally, be committed to – the aims of corporate security. 'Population management' refers to the deployment of techniques (security gates, barriers, identity cards, CCTV, alarms, access control systems, etc.) directed towards the observation, containment, control or exclusion of persons operating inside or outside the organisation. 'Information management' refers, at one level, merely to techniques directed at controlling the misuse, abuse or loss of corporate information. However, the management of information – its collection, collation, processing and re-processing as 'intelligence' – is fundamental to all present-day security practices and, for that reason, intelligence management, rather than being a separate category from the other two, is also inscribed within each. In the following section we explore the impact of risk-based thinking outside the corporate domain using this classification as a basis for the analysis of key developments.

## Risk management outside the corporate sphere

### Background

In the previous section we emphasised that insurance and risk minimisation were fundamental to the historical development of capitalist enterprise. In this section we consider the impact of risk-based thinking on the state and civil society with particular reference to the administration of security and justice. Initially, two sets of observations may be made about these developments. The first concerns the development of 'police science' and the historical emergence of the modern (or 'new') police. McMullan notes that up until the eighteenth century, 'police was primarily preoccupied with re-fixing communal relations' (1998). With the impact of Enlightenment thinking, however, 'the object of police shifted from the conservation of society to the bio-political care of life' (ibid.: 104). Accordingly, the focus of police changed from a reactive to a future-oriented one and police became 'a method for the analysis of a population living in a territory' (Foucault cited in ibid.: 104).

This orientation towards 'the analysis of a population living in a territory' bears a remarkable similarity to the corporate (risk-based) mentality described earlier. After all, effective risk-management demands the production of accurate knowledge about persons occupying a given (corporate) space. Yet, this similarity is hardly surprising since, as we said in Chapter 4, the preventive police model grew not from a state initiative but from a private one, Patrick Colquhoun's Thames River Police predating the Metropolitan force by nearly thirty years. Neither does the similarity end there. As McMullan (1998) shows, Colquhoun's police science employed a variety of preventive techniques including the statistical division of the population into discrete socio-economic categories; the conjoining of police and Poor Law institutions through the establishment of a 'pauper police'; the establishment of a registry of lodging houses and their occupants; the development of a compendium of criminal offenders; and the establishment of a centrally-organised intelligence service supplemented by a system of paid informants.

Though, for much of the twentieth century, this preventive orientation was undermined by the police's growing commitment to detection (Morn, 1982) and bandit-catching (Brogden and Shearing, 1993), the same preventive thrust has re-emerged in recent years. Indeed, Colquhoun's deployment of surveillance techniques and interagency 'partnerships' in combination with methodologies of 'human science' is strikingly similar to contemporary techniques. In that respect, his demand for a surveillance-based police science founded upon 'constant vigilance and attention' (Colquhoun cited in McMullan, 1998: 105) presages the use of video-surveillance, geographical information systems and behavioural profiling.

As in Colquhoun's day, contemporary thinking is directed towards the broad problem of governance rather than the narrow problem of crime. Consider contemporary policy initiatives directed at the issue of social exclusion. In Britain, the Labour government is committed to addressing the problem at central, regional and local levels. Clearly, such a strategy demands the collection of reliable data so that policy may be targetted at those in areas of greatest need. Recently, a colleague of one of us attended a conference at which a local authority representative outlined the methodology of data collection in his city. Here, partnerships established between local government departments and statutory and voluntary bodies ensured the widest possible sharing of information. Aggregate data about rates of educational achievement, school performance, life expectancy, morbidity and mortality, criminal offending, criminal victimisation and so on could be cross-tabulated for city, district and ward levels. More than that, however, specific data on individuals and their families could also be generated for single streets, for groups of houses in single streets and, ultimately, for single households.

This example is important not only because of the ethical issues it raises – not least the question of how to balance 'privacy' with 'social needs' – but because it demonstrates a governmental project comparable in scope and complexity to those formulated during the era of the 'Victorian administrative state'. The mentality of data collection displayed in the example – systematic, exact, universal *and* particular – mirrors the aspirations displayed by governing authorities during the era of 'inspection fervour' in late nineteenth-century Britain. These aspirations are well-captured in the following observation made by Steedman: 'Carried away by the vision of a thoroughly policed and inspected society, some, including county chief constables, suggested that the homes of the poor should be inspected by the police, for cleanliness and against overcrowding' (1984: 54). There are two main differences between Victorian aspirations and those of the present. First, while Victorian social reformers lacked the technical means to further many of their regulatory aims, present-day technologies – some of which we discuss more fully below – offer somewhat greater scope for governing the future. Second, while the Victorian regulatory programme was predicated upon the omnipresence of the state, the regulatory regimes of the present draw upon a variety of governing authorities (or 'partners').

A second issue concerns the impact of legal relations on the philosophy and practice of risk minimisation. Here, two observations may be made. Earlier we noted that risk-based thinking had an uneven impact on public policing. While Colquhoun's preventive experiment provided the inspiration for the new police, it was the philosophy and practice of bandit catching, rather than that of risk minimisation, which prevailed for much of the twentieth century. One factor in this was the differential impact of law on the policing of public and private property. In private places – such as the warehouses protected by Colquhoun's Marine Police Establishment or the shopping malls protected by today's security guards – social relations are underpinned by contracts and the specific conditions defined therein. For example, those seeking access to private places – whether as workers or as customers – may have to waive rights they would normally possess as citizens in public places. Under such conditions, private police may have the legal authority to exercise powers that they would not be able exercise publicly. In public places, by contrast, rights-bearing citizens make no such trade-offs and the police are constrained by legal rules protecting the rights and liberties of individual citizens. Historically, then, laws protecting citizens in public places made the exercise of risk-based policing by state police problematical. In the last half of the twentieth century this position began to change, the advent of mass private property facilitating the deployment of risk-based practices by public and private security organisations alike.

Thinking back to our previous conceptual discussion, it should also be said that the emergence of mass private property – typically in the form of shopping malls and 'gated' communities – facilitates the implementation of population management. Here, the underlying rationale is to observe, contain, control and, if necessary, exclude persons and things deemed 'bad', 'mad', 'dangerous', 'unruly', 'undesirable' or merely 'unfamiliar' from a given location. A recent analysis of gated communities in the USA captures the essential elements of this development: 'The residents of gated communities seek security, but more broadly they seek control. They want to control crime and traffic. They want to be free from strangers, disruptions, intrusions. They want privacy, stability, peace of mind, familiarity' (Blakely and Snyder, 1997: 143). Like Colquhoun's nineteenth-century project, this one also demands that 'police' – whether security guards or merely observant residents – come to 'know' the population policed (McMullan, 1998). By 'knowing' the characteristics and habits of those having legitimate access to the community, police are able to draw a categorical distinction between 'insiders' (good risks) and 'outsiders' (bad risks). In the second part of this section we discuss some other examples of risk-based practices undertaken outside the corporate domain, paying particular attention to developments in security and justice. In Chapter 6 we look at the wider significance of these developments by focusing on 'community policing' and 'partnership'.

### Risk management, security and justice

One critical factor in the adoption of proactive security measures by civil and state agents has simply been the increased availability of sophisticated preventive technologies. Consider the use of genetic and biometric techniques. In 1999 the British Home Secretary, Jack Straw, announced plans to allow the police to store DNA samples obtained from innocent people in the course of police investigations. Previously, legislation had stipulated that DNA taken from an individual during the course of mass screening must be destroyed once that individual was eliminated from the investigation in question. By the late 1990s 120 mass screenings in Britain had produced more than 400,000 DNA samples at a cost of £40 each. In addition, some 600,000 samples from convicted offenders were stored on the National DNA Database (Sparrow, 1999). Apart from reasons of cost, the rationale put forward in the Home Secretary's proposals (Home Office, 1999b) consisted of two elements. One related to the fact that 'certain individuals will fit the profile of possible suspects in more than one investigation and may therefore be approached a number of times in mass screening exercises' (ibid.: para. 50). In this case the police had expressed concern that people might refuse to give samples if approached on successive occasions. A second reason put forward related to the Home Secretary's desire to bring the law into line with current technological developments in furtherance of effective policing – something for which there was already precedent:

> In 1984 PACE [the Police and Criminal Evidence Act] limited the taking of body samples to people suspected of 'serious arrestable offences', for example rape and murder, and where it was relevant to the offence under investigation. With the development of DNA profiling it was clear that the law had to be updated to ensure that the investigation of crime derived the maximum benefit from DNA. The Criminal Justice and Public Order Act 1994 therefore amended PACE to extend the circumstances in which body samples may be taken and made possible the operation of a National DNA Database.
>
> (ibid.: para. 45)

In order to meet these conditions it was proposed that Section 64 of PACE be amended to permit the retention and use of samples, and the information derived from them, with the volunteer's written consent. Home Office Circular 25/2001 (Home Office, 2001b) confirms these changes and outlines the new wording which police forces should employ when taking DNA samples. Where individuals agree to their sample being retained at the end of a case, the following consent is signed:

> I consent to my DNA sample and information derived from it being retained and used for purposes related to the prevention and detection of crime, the investigation of an offence or the conduct of a prosecution. I understand that this sample may be used in a speculative search (i.e. checks may be made against other DNA records held by or on behalf of relevant law enforcement authorities). I understand that once I have given my consent for the sample to be retained and used I cannot withdraw this consent.
>
> (ibid.: annex A)

The rationale that law should shadow technology is a particularly interesting one given the speed and scope of technical change. Biometric technology – which enables individuals to be identified by characteristics such as fingerprints, voice-prints and facial features – has obvious preventive potential in securing buildings, computer systems and electronic commercial transactions. One developing system uses the uniqueness of the human iris – no two of which are alike – for security purposes. Cameras capable of photographing customer's eyes have now been installed into automatic telling machines at various US banks, replacing the traditional PIN number as a means of accessing accounts. However, scanning technology has a much wider potential. One of the companies involved in developing iris recognition systems plans to set up scan terminals in subways and at train stations in order to control commuters' access to platforms. As one industry spokesman put it: 'The uses for iris recognition pretty much span anything where someone needs to be identified . . . it's quick, it's reliable, it's easy to use. When you consider cost, risk reduction and privacy protection, it turns out to be quite affordable' (cited in Miller, 1999). Of course, the preventive potential of such scanning systems is magnified once they are integrated with other complementary systems. Such system integration would enable individuals and groups considered 'high risk' to be excluded from locations such as malls, station platforms, airports and university campuses, or to have limits placed upon their access.

One technology that has clear potential for integration with others is the so-called 'smart tag'. Up to now, tags have been used, primarily, to control shoplifting in stores. They may now be hidden in credit cards and company identification cards, as well as within normal merchandise. Data from the new generation of tags will be picked up by radio waves without the knowledge or consent of the person bearing the tag (Holcomb, 1999). Consequently, tags offer huge potential to employers wishing to monitor the activities of their staff. In addition, shops, banks and other businesses will be able to 'look inside' people's purses and wallets to elicit personal information about consumption preferences and the like. Such data may then be used to make proactive decisions about purchasing, staffing, investment or marketing. Tags may also be integrated with video-surveillance systems and DNA databanks for security purposes.

A further development is the functional integration of elements within a single location. 'Intelligent buildings' are already a reality in some parts of the corporate sector, but similar developments will spread to the domestic sphere. As more and more individuals set up 'home offices' and incorporate hi-tech audio and visual equipment into their houses, it is likely that there will be an increased demand for integrated networking systems. Some companies already offer services in this area. The IBM Home Director package is marketed as the ultimate in 'intelligent home' technology, the basic components of the system integrating the functions of heating, ventilation, air conditioning, computer, phone, lights and security (Pelletier, 1999).

Of course, surveillance is a fundamental component of all preventive activity. A survey by the American Management Association found that 32.8 per cent of major US companies record and review employee communications and activities (McGill, 1999). In Chapter 4 we referred to the growth of CCTV cameras in British towns and cities. Alongside this, there has been a proliferation of speed cameras on roads. Recently, a new surveillance system came into operation on the M1 catching 4,300 offenders in a single day. The Speed Violation Detection Deterrent (SVDD) that was approved for use on 1 April 1999 (Home Office, 1999c) is a digital system using no film or radar. When triggered, it records the date, time, location and speed of the car, providing a full colour image of the front of the vehicle including number plate, manufacturer, model and colour. Of course, such developments in surveillance are not restricted to public places. In Toronto, one area of growth in demand for surveillance cameras has come from parents wanting to spy on their children's nannies. A spokesman for one company operating in this field – Family Watch – stated that of the hundreds of nannies spied on in the Metro area, 90 per cent are fired for incompetence or worse. Recently, a 24-year-old babysitter was charged with assaulting a child after being filmed by a hidden camera and Toronto police predict that charges against babysitters will become commonplace (Payne, 1999).

The techniques described here and in previous pages should not be considered in isolation. New surveillance technologies are both the product of a risk-based mentality and a condition of its growing influence. One common feature of the risk-based approach is the assumption that actors exercise rational choice as a matter of routine. (Whether this assumption is necessary to risk-based thinking need not concern us for the moment.) This assumption is increasingly important in the field of criminal justice where risk has a growing influence on policy and practice. Take the example of criminal 'profiling', an idea which, through popular TV programmes like 'Cracker' has revolutionised people's ideas about police procedure. For the profiler there is no such thing as a random homicide. While crimes may seem to be motiveless, a discernible pattern may be identified: 'we can have the most pathological offender doing the most heinous acts to his victims but there still is a non-pathological method of looking for victims, hunting for them, and if we understand that we can work backwards' (Rossmo, 1998). Likewise, 'journey to crime research' shows that criminals tend to commit crimes fairly closely – though not too closely – to where they live. Drawing upon this, proponents of geographical profiling echo the views of corporate managers when they emphasise that 'the same patterns of behaviour . . . McDonalds will study when they're trying to determine where to place a new restaurant . . . also apply to criminals' (ibid.). Accordingly, profilers concentrate on the locations of crime, inputting co-ordinates, latitudes and longitudes into computer systems so as to generate probabilities about offender locations and likely crime 'hot spots'.

The growing influence of risk-based thinking is particularly apparent in the field of community corrections. In Britain, the probation service functioned, traditionally, as the rehabilitative and welfare arm of the criminal justice system. Questions of risk undoubtedly arose – as, for example, when serious offenders were released into the community after long prison sentences – but the main task of probation officers was to address the problematic behaviours and the personal and social problems of their clients: to 'advise, assist and befriend' as the originators of the service described it. Since the late 1980s, however, new legislation and policy direction have re-defined the service's role. Nowadays the principal task of probation officers is to target resources upon those individuals considered to constitute the greatest risk to society (Kemshall, n.d.).

Of course, this re-definition of community corrections is by no means peculiar to Britain. In North America, where developments are probably more advanced than in Britain, new technologies have been developed to assist with the task. In the USA, automated software programmes for offender risk assessment/management have been available for some time. The Northpointe Institute for Public Management, established in 1997, manufactures one such programme, COMPAS (Correctional Offender Management Profiling for Alternative Sanctions), a 'Computerised Risk Assessment for Community Placement'. COMPAS 2.0 is 'a fully automated broad band assessment covering a multi-dimensional set of well known criminogenic factors' (COMPAS 2.0, 1999). The product may assist in all areas of offender management including pre-trial release, pre-sentence investigation, probation supervision, prison parole release decisions, parole case management, and the screening of community corrections and intermediate sanctions. The manufacturers claim that COMPAS 2.0 is applicable to offenders at all levels of seriousness from 'non-violent misdemeanants to repeat violent felons'. The system can assist in determining an offender's appropriateness for community placement and, having done so, can specify corresponding levels of supervision and/or treatment. Each of its four 'risk potential scales' (violence, recidivism, flight and community non-compliance) has a reliability coefficient above 0.70, thereby confirming 'highly satisfactory psychometric reliabilities'. Using psychometric scaling models the system is also able to assess the broad areas of criminal involvement, social environment, pro-criminal sentiments, criminogenic needs and psychopathy/psychological factors. COMPAS 3.0, the most recent version of the software, has several new refinements including validity checks that warn against the likelihood of offenders lying or responding randomly to questions. In addition, the programme has four new 'higher order scales', all of which are said to be based upon relevant academic research: socialisation failures (inspired by Lykken's work on family problems as a precursor to sociopathy and criminality); criminal opportunity (drawing upon Cohen and Felson's routine activities theory and Sampson and Laub's work on continuity and desistance with respect to crime); criminal personality (building upon the work of Eysenck and of Bandura); and social supports (inspired by Hirschi's work in social control theory and Horney *et al.*'s analysis of social bonding as a factor in crime reduction). The application of these various techniques enable COMPAS to provide a comprehensive case summary relating to each offenders 'Overall Risk Potential' and 'Criminogenic and Needs Profile', calculated as a percentage and graded 'low', 'medium' or 'high' risk/need (COMPAS 3.0, 2000). The manufacturers claim that the system is easy to operate and may be configured by its users in no more than twenty minutes. It has the capacity to produce risk and need reports in less than ten seconds.

The deployment of risk-based techniques in the management of offenders – and, more generally, in the wider fields of crime prevention and community safety – raises several issues. First, the approach demands the systematic collection, collation, analysis and dissemination of information. For that reason, considerable emphasis is placed upon the development of collaborative relations between the different 'partners' who may assist in this process. In Britain, it is argued that the management and supervision of sexual offenders in the community demands close co-operation between the probation and police services, local authorities, social workers, voluntary agencies and others. One of the main preconditions of good risk management is thus said to be effective information exchange between participants, something which implies the development of 'common computerised and integrated recording systems for cases' (Association of Chief Officers of Probation cited in Hebenton and Thomas, 1996: 434). This move towards 'informatised' (Hebenton and Thomas, 1995) and 'communication'-based (Ericson and Haggerty, 1997) organisations has profound implications, one of which concerns the capacity of such organisations to process effectively vast amounts of information. Some of the other implications of these developments are discussed in a police context in Chapter 6.

A second question concerns the status of the information used in risk management. This issue was illustrated recently in Britain after the joint publication of a consultation paper, *Managing Dangerous People with Severe Personality Disorder* (London: Home Office/Department of Health, 1999). The document is concerned with the challenge to public safety posed by the small minority of people whose personality disorder is sufficiently severe to constitute a risk to public safety. It is estimated that just over 2,000 people fall into this category in England and Wales. Of that number, over 98 per cent are men, the vast majority of whom reside in prisons or secure hospitals. The paper notes that present day law fails to protect the public from the risks posed by these individuals since it may permit their return to the community even when they remain dangerous. The document notes that 'research into the causes of severe personality disorder, and into how best to address the associated risks, has been inconclusive'. It adds, however, that while the results of new research are awaited, 'decisions on the direction of policy development for managing this group cannot be delayed until the outcomes of the research are known' (ibid.). The document puts forward two alternative policy options for consideration. The first would strengthen existing legislation so that dangerous people with severe personality disorders (DSPD) would not be released from prison or hospital while they continued to present a risk to the public. This option, which would allow for greater use to be made of the discretionary life sentence, would build on existing service structures both in prisons (for offenders) and in secure mental health facilities (for civil detainees). The second would introduce a new legal framework providing powers for the indeterminate detention of DSPD individuals in both criminal and civil proceedings and for their supervision and recall following release from detention. For these purposes a new specialist service would be set up for the management of DSPD individuals separate from, but having close links with, the prison and health services. As a result of the consultation process the Home Affairs Committee has strongly recommended the second option. Coupled with this, the government has invested £70 million into pilot projects concerned to establish a rigorous assessment tool and effective forms of treatment for DSPD (Home Office, 2000).

We shall discuss the issue of risk assessment in respect of 'dangerous' populations further in Chapter 6. However, two issues raised in the consultation paper are worthy of note. First, it is recognised that, for either set of proposals to be implemented effectively, it would be necessary to have better trained and supervised workers in post, new monitoring arrangements in place, and better communication and closer working arrangements between the various partner agencies. Second, while insisting that risk management and risk assessment techniques are now 'developing scientifically both within the criminal justice system and the health service' the document admits that 'at the present time it is considerably easier to assess risk within the short term rather than the longer term' (Home Office/Department of Health, 1999). These two issues – the first relating to the efficacy of risk-based techniques and the second to the very validity of risk-based knowledge – provoked a heated debate after the document's publication. In particular, organisations such as the civil liberties pressure group, Liberty, cited experts who questioned whether those with 'severe personality disorders' could, in fact, be identified with the accuracy or consistency sufficient to justify the introduction of indeterminate sentences.

Whether these reservations are justified or not, the debate points to a fundamental problem concerning the status of expert knowledge in risk management. As various writers have pointed out (Giddens, 1990; Beck, 1992) the public's demand for expert knowledge in risk management is often accompanied by their lack of trust in the very solutions proposed for managing risks. This points to a third issue, regarding the paradoxical relationship between security and risk. As Hebenton and Thomas's (1996) analysis of sexual offenders in the community implies, it is not merely a question of whether risk-based initiatives 'work' – as, for example in debates about the effectiveness of partnership arrangements – the very techniques are paradoxical. In the USA residents can now click on the home page of local police forces and download information (including address, offence category, ethnic category, and age of victim) on named sexual offenders living within the local precinct area. As an extra bonus, they are also presented with a 'mug-shot' of the offender. Such developments reflect recent legislation giving citizens the right to be notified of sexual offenders living in their localities. No doubt these developments will empower citizens, making them feel more secure. But, they also breed insecurity: about the reliability of available information; about the trustworthiness of the expert knowledge upon which it is based; and about the capacity of 'rational' offenders to evade disclosure.

## Risk and the punishment paradigm

How does the risk-based paradigm described in this chapter relate to the punishment-based one described previously? The aim of the punishment paradigm, in its utilitarian guise, is to govern through the will, usually but not invariably, via the body. For will-based governance to be feasible, of course, certain assumptions have to be made about human behaviour. Of these, the most fundamental is that human subjects possess the capacity to discriminate rationally, and freely, between alternative actions and decisions. In other words, the model assumes that rational individuals exercise choice – in much the same way as business corporations do – by making successive cost–benefit calculations. Punishment, that is, the application and removal of pain, seeks to exert influence on the way subjects exercise that free choice. The rational offender will seek to balance the economic benefits accruing from, say, the theft of stolen car radios with the likely costs arising from apprehension and punishment. In addition to that, states – assumed by the model to be mere aggregations of human subjects – will also possess a capacity for rational action. For that reason, 'classical' proponents of the punishment paradigm called upon governing authorities to calibrate pain according to rational principles. In Beccaria's view, pain was only to be applied sufficiently, and no more than was warranted, by the seriousness of the punishable action. The punishment paradigm is also inextricably linked to liberal notions of liberty and freedom. It demands that governments influence subject's actions by the rational application of pain, but it also demands that they respect subject's freedom of choice, including their freedom to act criminally. For that reason the punishment paradigm is an attempt to 'govern through freedom' (Rose, 1999).

Two observations may be made about this notion of government through freedom. First, it may be distinguished from so-called 'positivist' approaches to governance. While the Beccarian approach defines offenders as self-contained, culpable free agents, the positivist one regards their free choice as constrained by external (social, psychological or genetic) factors. While the first places emphasis on punishment, deterrence and just deserts for offenders, the second stresses the need for their welfare, care, rehabilitation and treatment. Finally, while the first espouses the value of proportionate and determinate sentences, the second accepts the legitimacy of indeterminate ones. The essential difference between these two approaches is encapsulated in the distinction between 'reform' and 're-qualification'. For positivists – as, indeed, for some classical theorists, such as Bentham, for whom certain punishments were potentially reformative – the object of pain was to reform the subject. In the twentieth century this reformist approach has been exemplified in the rehabilitative model where sentences are tailored to the needs of particular offenders, something which conflicts with 'the notion of a right not to be punished disproportionately' (Ashworth, 1997: 1099). By contrast, Beccarian punishment is, to use Foucault's phrase, directed at 'a juridical subject in the process of re-qualification' (Rose, 1999). Such punishment, especially when seen from a just deserts perspective, is of fixed duration and is proportionate to the seriousness of the offence. Furthermore, once the punishment is completed, the offender has the legitimate right, like any other free citizen, to re-join society. This process is analogous to the regulation of certain contact sports. Players in these sports routinely choose ('freely') to break the rules in order to secure some illegitimate advantage over their opponents. Accordingly, the rules of most contact sports define 'fouls' as deliberate (freely chosen) actions, an 'accidental foul' being a literal contradiction in terms. Drawing upon the sporting analogy, Bottoms (1983) provides an illuminating account of this process of re-qualification. Beccarian punishment, he suggests, involves processes similar to those occurring in ice-hockey matches. Players who break the rules during games may receive a penalty (a 'time-out') of fixed duration during which they are required to leave the ice. As part of their punishment they are allocated a position in a separate area, at the side of the ice, symbolically separated from other team members. By this means, the infraction is marked for all to see, the aim being to deter other players from committing similar offences. Critically, however, once the recalcitrant player has sat out the required time penalty, he is permitted to return to the ice as a fully 're-qualified subject'.

However, a second issue also has to be considered. In practice, governance through freedom (or 'punishment through choice') may be combined with other governmental techniques so as to produce hybrid forms. In Chapter 3 we described the problems associated with the attempt to implement Beccaria's classical model of sentencing in the French Penal Code of 1791. Judges, finding it difficult to adhere strictly to the principle of proportionality between offence and punishment, regardless of the background and circumstances of the offender, secured more and more discretion in sentencing. The result was the so-called 'neoclassical' compromise whereby extraneous factors (age, mental capacity, intent, etc.) could be introduced to minimise or maximise culpability.

The existence of hybrid forms is no less apparent today. Take the case of imprisonment. Imprisonment, like any sanction, can be informed by competing penal mentalities. For classical theorists prison was an arena for the re-qualification of free (offending) subjects. (In that context, prison is an ironic technology, celebrating freedom while, simultaneously, restricting it.) For positive theorists prison was an arena for diagnosing offenders' needs and initiating open-ended programmes for their reform. In recent years, however, the decline of the reformist ethic has meant that the long-standing dialogue between re-qualification and reform has given way to a new one linking re-qualification with 'incapacitation'. Incapacitation aims to identify those who are likely to offend in the future and, having done so, to invoke protective measures – usually lengthy periods of imprisonment – against them. The approach adopts no particular behavioural premise about offenders – though it does assume a capacity for rational action on the part of governing authorities – being concerned exclusively with the minimisation of future harms by the application of utilitarian means. Recent examples of the deployment of the incapacitive approach would include 'three strikes and you're out' in the USA and the use of 'public protection' sentences under the terms of the Criminal Justice Act 1991 in Britain. The expansion of prison populations in many jurisdictions is linked to the growing significance of incapacitation. In turn, the growing significance of incapacitation is linked to the transfer of risk-based thinking from the corporate to the state sector of governance. As a governing practice, incapacitation differs from both reform and re-qualification. Where the former acts on subject's (physical, social and psychological) constitutions and the latter acts on their wills, incapacitation merely aims to manipulate the conditions that might give rise to harm. As such, incapacitation is a managerial technique for minimising risks.

How, then, might we sum up the relationship between the old paradigm of punishment and the new paradigm of risk? Under the punishment paradigm, pain has the dual purpose of governing the past and governing the future. Pain for the purpose of retribution is meant to guarantee justice (by 'making good' for past offences). Pain for the purpose of deterrence is meant to guarantee security (by 'making safe' from future ones). Now, it is clear that the paradigm is open to empirical criticism. Studies of recidivism suggest that the goals of security are poorly served by deterrence, while evidence from victimology suggests that the rights of victims are poorly served by retribution. Yet, despite that, the paradigm has obvious strengths. On the one hand, a rigorous distinction is drawn between security and justice at the conceptual level. (Not only are the terms conceptually distinct, their location in separate time dimensions also gives them temporal specificity.) On the other hand, the paradigm is able to provide an integrated theory of the substantive relationship between the two. For all of its shortcomings, then, the paradigm demonstrates parsimony and order.

This is far from true of the developments described in the present chapter. Whereas punishment offers an integrated method – albeit a flawed one – for governing the past and the future, the risk paradigm seems to have de-coupled the former, entirely, from the latter. Thus, while many states deploy the punishment paradigm more and more vigorously in governing the past (justice) – as evidenced, particularly, by escalating prison populations in the USA – responsibility for governing the future (security) is increasingly devolved to corporate and civil agents who are well versed in the principles of risk management . Yet, that is only part of the picture. As we have demonstrated in this chapter, states not only engage in punishment (for purposes of justice) and in the devolution of preventive responsibility (for purposes of security), they also deploy risk-based practices (for purposes of *both* security and justice).

Consider the so-called 'Scruffy Case' in Kansas. Here, two young men were convicted of the severe maltreatment and killing of a dog ('Scruffy') and sentenced to twenty-two months in jail, followed by probation. The case raised considerable controversy since experts maintained that the profile of many convicted murderers revealed them to have previously inflicted cruelty on animals. In the light of this risk-based evidence, the sentence in the 'Scruffy' case had a two-fold rationale: to punish the youths for the offence they had committed; and, by incapacitating them, to minimise the risk of their committing a comparable offence against humans in the future. What this example shows is that the risk paradigm not only de-couples governing the past (justice) from governing the future (security), it also conflates the very distinction between security and justice which was so central to the punishment paradigm. The mechanism for this conflation is simple. By defining justice in futuristic (or 'anticipatory') terms, its exclusive equation with governing the past ('making good') is breached. The 'Scruffy' case, like similar examples described earlier in the chapter, defines justice both in terms of retribution and in terms of security. In the latter respect, 'making good' *is* 'making safe'.

This means that the relationship between the risk paradigm and the punishment paradigm is more complex and multi-faceted than Garland's dualistic (1996) analysis would suggest. In Garland's view, the punishment of crime (justice) is a necessary state monopoly while the control of crime (security) is, increasingly, devolved – though he has reservations about for how long – to 'responsibilised' civil agents. We suggest that a more complicated process is at work: one in which the paradigm of risk both de-couples the governance of the past (justice) from the governance of the future (security) and, simultaneously, re-integrates them in new combinations. The result may be a system that is increasingly effective in achieving security (by virtue of its focus on risk minimisation) but less effective in achieving justice (by virtue of its combination of retributive and anticipatory elements).

Two things may be said in conclusion. First, the growing influence of anticipatory justice raises a normative problem: when (if ever) is its application justified and within what limits? (For example, may one apply it legitimately to paedophiles but not to shoplifters? To those with 'serious' personality disorders rather than those with merely 'minor' ones?) Second, the system we have described no longer comprises the integrated and parsimonious package of old, the principles of retribution and risk being uneasy bedfellows. This begs another question. If we are to rely on the risk paradigm for the future provision of security, what model of justice is required to run alongside and complement it? How, in other words, might we construct an integrated theory of governing the past and governing the future, alternative to the punishment paradigm? We return to this question in the final chapter.

# 6

# ZERO-TOLERANCE,
# COMMUNITY POLICING
# AND PARTNERSHIP

## Introduction

Two developments in governance have had a major influence on the way in which security is promoted. First, there has been a shift towards instrumental forms of governance that focus attention less on the past and more on the future. Whereas, previously, governance was preoccupied with what happened in the past (a major concern of criminal justice discourse) it is now oriented, more and more, to the promotion of the future. Of course, this shift is by no means an absolute one. We are not claiming that established forms of governance are unconcerned about the future: continued debates about the efficacy of deterrence within criminal justice would confirm that that is not the case. Rather, there has been a shift in emphasis, so that issues of governance are, increasingly, 'made up' in terms of risk discourse. We can locate this shift across all terrains of governance, including the governance of security. Indeed the very term security reflects this future orientation since it focuses attention on the production of safety rather than on the resolution of past harms and wrongs.

Second, there has been a macroscopic shift in the way in which collective life is imagined and organised. Rose (1996), with deliberate overstatement, talks about the 'death of the social' and the 'birth of community' in drawing attention to this development. Evidence for this change can be found in the new language of collective life, with terms such as 'social justice', 'social problems' and 'social work' gradually being superseded by terms such as 'community justice', 'community problems' and 'community work'. The increased salience of the term 'community' signifies two things: that collective life is 'made up' in new ways; and that the spaces in which collective life is played out are becoming fractured and decentred. The metaphor of 'neo-feudalism' has been used to describe how collective space and collective living are fractured by the emergence of 'mass private property' (Shearing and Stenning, 1981, 1984, 1987). Perhaps the most obvious example of this development is the emergence of 'gated communities', that is, the 'fortified fragments' (Caldiera, 1996) within which people live, work and play. Such fragmented spaces include residential developments, industrial parks, commercial shopping areas, offices and recreational complexes. Often, these spaces are constituted through arrangements whereby the various occupants (residents, workers, customers and the like) enter contracts that specify the terms under which they will relate to each other and to the authorities that regulate them. For example, when buyers purchase a home in a gated community, the purchase agreement will specify the constitutional arrangements that will apply to them as community members. These developments suggest a massive re-feudalisation of collective life, one corollary of which has been that a variety of governmental functions once associated with the state – from garbage collection to policing – are now provided by 'private governments' (Mcauley, 1986). The provision of security is one of the most visible features of this re-feudalisation of governance.

These changes are directly linked to the historical shifts described previously. In Chapter 4 we noted that the contemporary re-adoption of Peel's preventive dream has involved various community-based reforms including an increased emphasis being placed on citizens as fully-fledged partners of the police; an increased involvement by non-specialised public, commercial and voluntary agencies in security governance; and, in accordance with these changes, an increased conflation of the, hitherto distinct, spheres of 'the governing' and 'the governed'. Alongside these community-oriented changes, risk-based modes of thought and action challenge the traditional view that deterrence is the principle means for achieving effective security governance. In accordance with this, agencies of security governance, such as the police, become more and more preoccupied with instrumental practices such as 'problem-oriented policing'. However, while this focus denies the Hobbesian/ Beccarian view that governance must be rooted in punishment, it neither claims that the imposition of pain, through the application of coercive technologies, is necessarily ineffective nor that it is inherently wrong. On the contrary, pain is now conceived – in suitably instrumental form – as one of a number of means to be utilised in security governance. For this reason, we have argued that while a paradigm change has undoubtedly taken place within security governance, the coercive institutions and technologies traditionally associated with punishment have also been maintained, thereby incorporating pain as one governing resource among others. Within the new instrumental paradigm the governance of security is identified with the application of *any* means that will promote safety and security.

In this chapter we explore, in more detail, the attempt to combine community-based modes of security governance with instrumentally-oriented/risk-based ones through an examination of Zero-Tolerance Policing (ZTP). We choose this example because ZTP is the archetypal case of a governing programme predicated upon the successful marriage of prevention and pain. Yet, commentary on ZTP has failed to address this issue concentrating, instead, on a range of different considerations. Some commentators have focused on ZTP as the product of charismatic action by police managers engaged in a tough war against crime. Some have engaged in prolonged debate about the efficacy of ZTP as a crime reduction strategy. Others have claimed that, by focusing its attention on 'the usual suspects' (young males who frequent public space) ZTP is merely 'old wine in new bottles'. Yet others have contended that ZTP is the antithesis of 'genuine' (consensual) community policing because of its willingness to coerce through the application of overly vigorous enforcement methods. Our view, on the contrary, is that ZTP is a mode of community policing precisely *because* it uses coercive techniques in order to apply pain for preventive ends within a dispersed governmental context. While debates about the efficacy or propriety of ZTP are undoubtedly important, our aim in this chapter is more specific. In the first section we outline the limits of the existing debate on ZTP. The second section depicts ZTP as a risk-based, information or intelligence-led mode of community policing linked to wider visions of community safety and dispersed community governance. In order to do this we focus on a single example – ZTP in Middlesbrough, England – though, in so doing, we neither suggest that the vision is realised, nor that it is unproblematic. In the third and final section we examine ZTP's use of coercive (pain-inducing techniques) for preventive ends by examining the New York experience. Here two things are emphasised: that common aims ('taking back the streets') may have different connotations in different places; and that ZTP is one of a variety of techniques used to deal with problems arising from the regulation of mass private spaces.

## The limits of the ZTP debate

Popular and academic debate about ZTP, though plentiful, has been limited in scope. Four types of considerations have, so far, dominated debate.

### ZTP as an heroic moral crusade

Readers of a certain age may be familiar with the 1950s American western series *The Lone Ranger*. During the course of each episode, the hero – a former Texas Ranger forced to wear a mask in order to hide his identity – succeeds in righting a serious injustice. Aiding him in this task are his trusty white horse (Silver) and his faithful Native American sidekick Tonto. Each episode ends with the same scene. As our hero rides off into the distance, one townsperson asks 'Who *was* that masked man' to which another replies 'That was the Lone Ranger'. A simple semiotic underlies this programme. The victim is invariably weak and in need of protection. The hero wears a white hat and rides a white horse. The villain wears a black hat and rides a black horse. The hero's task is to defeat the villain and, by so doing, to right wrongs and to re-impose moral order over situations of normative uncertainty.

Our reason for referring to this example is that popular depictions of ZTP in both New York and Middlesbrough bore striking comparison to a western morality play. In each case an heroic individual, albeit – unlike the self-effacing Lone Ranger – a self-proclaimed one, stepped forward to rid the community of wrongdoers. The initiator of ZTP in New York, William Bratton, declared in an article several years ago that 'Crime is down in New York City: blame the police' (Bratton, 1997). Bratton's view of his own contribution to this success was well captured in the title of his book *Turnaround: How America's Top Cop Reversed the Crime Epidemic* (Bratton, 1998). In Middlesbrough, Detective Superintendent Ray Mallon fulfilled a similar heroic role. When appointed Head of Middlesbrough CID in 1996 he had stated that if crime did not fall by 20 per cent within eighteen months he and his two detective inspectors would ask to be relieved of their duties. Mallon – pictured on the front cover of *Reader's Digest* under the headline 'Is this man Britain's toughest cop'? and shown 'pumping iron' during a later TV documentary – presented a consistently 'macho image' of ZTP. Not surprisingly, this proved popular with rank and file officers and with large sections of the Middlesbrough public. In effect, William Bratton and Ray Mallon were portrayed in the media as heroic 'white hats' leading a policing enterprise as morally unambiguous as that undertaken by *The Lone Ranger*.

## Ethical critiques of ZTP

The notion of ZTP as a moral mission assumes that 'good' overcomes 'bad', not by the use of silver bullets but by the police's zero-toleration of street-level law breaking and incivility. Usually, this policy is justified by the principles outlined in Wilson and Kelling's (1982) 'Broken Windows' thesis. Here it is argued that public toleration of routine minor incivilities on the street – window breaking, vandalism, aggressive begging, drunkenness, public urination and the like – increases 'respectable fears', encourages a spiral of community decline and, in the longer term, increases the risk of more serious crime occurring. Thus, in New York, police were ordered to arrest peddlers, drunks, vandals and others committing those 'quality of life' offences which were likely to precipitate community decline. By so doing, it was claimed, crime in New York fell by unprecedented levels and good prevailed.

However, critics have maintained that such robust activity encourages and sanctions police violence and discrimination. On 4 February 1999 Amadou Diallo, a Guinean with no criminal record, was challenged outside his Bronx apartment building by four plain-clothes members of the New York Police Department's 'Street Crime Unit' who were looking for a rape suspect. When challenged Diallo reached for his wallet. The police, believing he had a gun, opened fire and in the subsequent 41-shot fusillade, Diallo was hit by 19 bullets and killed. In February 2000 the four officers were acquitted of all criminal charges.

## The efficacy of ZTP

The most controversial and widely discussed aspect of ZTP has concerned its impact and effectiveness, something which has provoked continued dispute (Chaudhary and Walker, 1996; Dixon, 1999; Grabosky, 1999; Johnston, 1997a; O'Mahony, 1997; Pollard, 1997; Potter, 1996; Read, 1997). Consider the issue of reduced crime in New York. Here, critics have made several claims: that reductions in crime were related to declining crack cocaine use; to a reduction in the size of the young male population; and to the fact that mandatory sentencing had already removed many criminals from the streets; that organisational factors (including management reforms, the application of information technology and the deployment of increased numbers of police officers) were, primarily, responsible for any positive effects arising from the programme. It has also been suggested that other US jurisdictions – such as San Diego (Pollard, 1997) – have enjoyed similar reductions in recorded crime, using very different policing methodologies. In addition, it has been argued that ZTP might produce a range of negative effects: a rapid and costly expansion in the size of the prison population; a serious reduction in the scope of police officer discretion; a withdrawal of police officers from concentration on more serious crimes; and a dangerous targetting of ethnic and other minority populations which might, in turn, lead to a major deterioration in police–public relations. Finally, it has been claimed that officers in New York and Middlesbrough acted corruptly in order to place ZTP in a positive light. At one time in Middlesbrough 48 officers were under investigation accused of 430 alleged offences, two thirds of which related to criminal matters. Among these allegations, it was claimed that heroin was planted on suspects in police custody and also that officers gave heroin to users in return for information leading to the apprehension of user/dealers. Eight detectives, including Detective Superintendent Mallon were placed under suspension in 1997 while a lengthy and costly investigation (Operation Lancet) took place. In February 2001 the Crown Prosecution Service finally announced that none of the 400 criminal allegations investigated by Lancet against 60 officers would be proceeded with. At the time of writing, Cleveland Police continue to pursue internal disciplinary charges against Mallon who remains suspended.

### Conceptual disputes about ZTP

Two matters have been at issue. The first, which has been present in academic circles though less so in popular ones, has concerned the ownership of the term 'Zero-Tolerance'. Understandably, some feminists have expressed annoyance about the police's colonisation of the term (Campbell, 1997). The irony of this situation was particularly marked in Middlesbrough where the 'ZT' anti-domestic violence logo had been displayed on buses for a number of years prior to the implementation of ZTP. In 1997 a female reporter from the BBC Radio Four Today programme – who had spent several weeks in the area examining the popularity of ZTP and exploring alleged improprieties said to be associated with it –

annoyed feminists by commenting that 'even the buses in Middlesbrough carry the Zero Tolerance message'.

For present purposes, however, it is the second issue that is critical to our argument. So far, we have suggested a tendency among commentators to misrecognise the significance and character of ZTP. Undoubtedly, this has been most marked in popular debates where recognition of the complexity of ZTP has been overridden by an emphasis on its 'heroic' and 'moral' essence. Ironically, however, it is the heroes themselves who provide the strongest confirmation of disparity between the heroic and complex versions of ZTP. Both Ray Mallon and William Bratton have been surprisingly ambivalent about the term 'Zero Tolerance'. While ready to participate in the media frenzy that publicised ZTP, each preferred to use alternative terminology to describe what really happened. In Middlesbrough, Mallon talked about 'Confident Policing', 'Positive Policing' and 'Here and Now Policing'. Bratton went much further; claiming that what happened in New York was 'neither Zero-Tolerance Policing nor quality of life policing'. The significance of this comment was brought home to one of us at a conference attended by Bratton. Two things were apparent at this conference. First, all speakers addressing the audience (almost all of whom were senior police officers) distanced themselves from the terminology of 'Zero Tolerance'. Second, minimal reference was made to 'quality of life' issues. Instead, discussion centred on various matters relating to achieving effective crime management through the application of future-oriented preventive techniques. These included the assessment of crimes in terms of their 'detectability', the use of intelligence and informants, the targetting and profiling of offenders, the use of crime pattern analysis and geographical information systems, the identification of criminal 'hot-spots' and the disorganisation and disruption of criminal organisations.

For the remainder of this chapter we shall argue that ZTP is a complex and shifting combination of overlapping elements two of which are particularly important. First, while retaining elements of traditional enforcement-based policing, its central objective is to effect prevention through community-based multi-agency partnership. Second, while being committed to prevention, ZTP by no means shuns the application of pain in pursuing those preventive goals. On the contrary, pain becomes a key preventive mechanism. In order to consider the first of these points we shall examine the process by which ZTP evolved into 'Community Oriented Problem Solving' (COPS) in Middlesbrough.

## Information, prevention and partnership

Cleveland is a de-industrialised region in the North East of England whose past dependence on the declining steel and chemical industries has produced a lack of economic diversity, high levels of unemployment and an increasingly casualised labour market. Between 1975 and 1986 a quarter of all jobs were lost in the region, almost half of those people employed in manufacturing and construction being made redundant (Cleveland County Council, 1986). In June 1999 unemployment in the Teesside area of Cleveland stood at twice the national average of 4.3 per cent (JSU, 1999). In Middlesbrough, the largest town in the Teesside region, 10.7 per cent of people were officially unemployed, though the real 'jobless' total (including unemployed claimants, those on training schemes, and those 'economically inactive' who would take jobs if they were available) amounted to about 35 per cent. In addition to that, existing high levels of crime (notably burglary and car crime) had been exacerbated by the rapid expansion of heroin use. By 1997 Middlesbrough had the dubious distinction of having the cheapest heroin in Britain available on its streets. Such was the extent of the town's accumulated difficulties that the right-wing polemicist, Charles Murray, controversially identified Middlesbrough as the home of Britain's 'new rabble underclass' (Murray, 1994). The existence of these accumulated problems, combined with the appointment of Detective Superintendent Mallon as Head of Middlesbrough CID, led to the introduction of ZTP in 1996.

The principal aims of this policy (Mallon, 1997) were to reduce all recorded crime, particularly within the categories of house burglary, violence and car crime; to reduce fear of crime; to increase public confidence in and support of the police; and to increase police performance. In order to achieve these objectives three categories of offence were prioritised: house burglary, anti-social behaviour by young people (particularly the intimidation of passers-by and the riding of motor cycles and bicycles on pavements) and quality of life offences, such as dropping litter. The police responded to burglary in three ways: through the deployment of informants; through the instigation of proactive and covert operations; and through the operation of stop-checks. Anti-social behaviour and quality of life offences were dealt with by the police confronting offenders and, where necessary, asserting their authority over them.

Already, it is clear from this brief description of tactics employed, that the populist view of ZTP as a mere enforcement-led strategy is simplified. Take the example of stop-and-search, the most crucial component in the police's enforcement toolbox. Police in Middlesbrough undoubtedly employed stop-and-search powers to a considerable extent during this period. During 1998–9, for example, 48,513 stop-searches were recorded by Cleveland Police (a relatively small force of officers). This figure was only exceeded by four other forces in England and Wales, three of them being the large metropolitan ones of London, Greater Manchester and Merseyside. In fact, the Cleveland total represented a massive 101 stop-searches per 1,000 head of population: twice the total for any other force; more than two-and-a-half times the total for the London and Merseyside Metropolitan forces; more than four-times the total for the Manchester metropolitan force; and over nine times the total for the West Midlands metropolitan force. At first sight, these figures would seem to confirm that ZTP is, first and foremost, a robust enforcement-based strategy. However, when we consider the percentage of stop-searches culminating in an arrest, the picture changes dramatically. For, remarkably, in both 1997–8 and 1998–9 Cleveland achieved the lowest percentage of arrests from stop-searches (at, respectively, 6 and 7 per cent) of any of the forty-three police forces in England and Wales (figures derived from Home Office, 1999d: tables 3.1, 3.2 and 3.4).

One implication of this peculiar statistic is that the police's enforcement powers were used less for bandit-catching than for purposes of information gathering. Of course, this is no great discovery. Police have always used their formal-legal powers to facilitate the achievement of informal ends. What is striking in this case, however, is the scale of that exercise. Moreover, the official figures undoubtedly underestimate the quantity of informal 'trawling' which actually occurred in Middlesbrough. A Cleveland police officer, interviewed by one of us, drew a distinction between three activities undertaken in the town: 'stop-searches' (which deploy powers enshrined in the Police and Criminal Evidence Act 1984 and which are subject to the associated recording requirements and safeguards contained therein), 'stop-checks' (which may yield a voluntary search and which do not invoke PACE safeguards) and 'stop-talks' (a term which requires no further explanation).

In fact, the picture is even more complicated since, far from being a simple enforcement strategy, ZTP in Middlesbrough constituted an ensemble of four interrelated elements. First there was a short-term, enforcement-based strategy to 'win back the streets' from criminals and troublemakers. Second, running alongside this, was the police's discretionary use of their enforcement powers to effect stops for purposes of information gathering. Third was the police's decision to articulate ZTP with Problem-Oriented Policing (POP) – a decision dating back to the initial implementation of ZTP in 1996. Here, the principle was that, having first cleared the streets of troublemakers and then collected street-level information for purposes of intelligence production, an instrumentally-oriented problem-solving approach would next be implemented. Finally, this intelligence-led and problem-oriented approach was to be developed, not exclusively by the police, but by a plurality of local agencies contained within a community safety partnership.

Middlesbrough's *Strategy for Reducing Crime and Disorder 1999–2002* (Middlesbrough Crime and Disorder Steering Group, 1999) demonstrates clearly the links between ZTP, multi-agency partnerships and the design and deployment of information-based modes of preventive activity. The Strategy is organised through partnership arrangements between a number of constituent agencies including 'The Community Safety Forum' (made up of over 100 organisations including businesses, the voluntary sector, schools, the local university, Victim Support, Community Councils, the Youth Service, the Domestic Violence Forum, the Commission for Racial Equality and the Crown Prosecution Service), 'Task Groups' (including, among others, housing, domestic violence, prostitution, drugs, and youth), a 'Crime and Disorder Steering Group' (made up of the police, the police authority, the local council, and the health and probation services) and an 'Audit Group'. The role of the Task Groups, which contain a large number of professionals, is particularly interesting since, in due course, it is hoped they will become permanent partnerships functioning to provide 'a continuing source of advice and intelligence' (ibid.: 6).

The Strategy document identifies seven key aims for the period 1999–2002. For example, Key Aim 7 is 'To develop greater under-standing in order to reduce the levels of violence and discriminatory attitudes and behaviour towards vulnerable groups, while increasing the level of support for victims'. Having done that, it specifies a range of objectives, target outcomes and detailed action plans, together with a process for monitoring and evaluating their implementation. Each single activity outlined in the action plan will be the responsibility of a specific partner. Thus, for example, Objective 7.1 (of Key Aim 7) is 'To promote a pervading climate of Zero-Tolerance against discriminatory behaviour, language and attitudes which affects vulnerable people (based on gender, sexuality, religion, race, social status, mental health, disability and age)'. Several means are specified for achieving this single aim, each having a defined target and an accountable ('Lead') agency responsible for its delivery; for example,

> *Means*: by running campaigns and training especially in schools on all forms of discrimination and bullying
> *Targets*: to raise awareness of the negative and damaging effects of discrimination in all its forms
> *Lead Agency*: the Council.

Most important of all, the document notes that 'new ways of working' are being developed by the four statutory agencies (Police, Council, Health Authority and Probation). Based upon the principles of POP, the agencies have developed an approach, COPS, to local service delivery in Middlesbrough. This approach, it is hoped, would enable the agencies – particularly the Police and the Council – to work together with the community to address community needs more effectively by the use of shared premises, shared information, shared intelligence and shared technology. The important implication behind COPS is that agencies will *collectively* deliver their services from coterminous locations developing common practices of information collection, collation, processing, management, and exchange in the process of so doing. In this context, we might consider Gelsthorpe's (1985) attempt to differentiate between five different modes of partnership:

- *The Communication Model*: organisations recognise that they have a role to play with one another but go little beyond communication.
- *The Co-operation Model*: agencies maintain separate boundaries and identities but work together on a mutually-agreed problem.
- *The Co-ordination Model*: agencies work together in a systematic way, there are defined boundaries, and resources are pooled to tackle mutually-agreed problems.
- *The Federation Model*: agencies retain their organisational distinctiveness but also adopt degrees of central focus.
- *The Merger Model*: agencies become indistinguishable from one another in working on a mutually-defined problem.

Undoubtedly, the Middlesbrough strategy envisages multi-agency working as more than mere co-operation and co-ordination, its objective being to develop some genuinely 'federal' or 'merged' framework. In that regard, its conception of multi-agency partnership is strikingly similar to that implied in Ericson and Haggerty's (1997) research, the police and their partner agencies becoming information-based organisations within a local communications network. In addition to that, the community safety model implies that the functional distinction between partner agencies – the police's traditional concern with crime, as opposed to the schools' focus on education or the health authority's concentration on health care – becomes increasingly untenable. Indeed the demise of that traditional distinction is one of the factors that differentiates the generic concept of 'community safety' (and related ideas about future-oriented community governance) from the traditional, and much narrower, concept of crime prevention.

Of course, it would be naïve to ignore the fact that implementation problems may undermine attempts to establish functioning community safety partnerships, such as that in Middlesbrough. Gilling (2000) notes a number of issues in this regard: that the police's traditional domination over criminal information might lead them only to engage in partnerships on their own terms; that the specific aims and objectives of partner agencies may be difficult to reconcile with a generic community safety plan; and that reliance on consultative mechanisms to resolve discord between partners may be problematic. However, it is important to place the issues of partnership and community governance in their wider context. Thus, while there is evidence to suggest that the partnership aspects of community policing have been rendered problematic by the sorts of implementation problems identified (Jones, 1980; Gill and Thrasher, 1985; Bennett, 1994), police organisations throughout the world continue to commit themselves to community police reforms. Such commitment cannot be dismissed as mere rhetoric on the part of police (compare Klockars, 1991), the product of some co-ordinated conspiracy by police managers to obscure the more unsavoury aspects of police work. For whatever their limits, community police reforms, such as ZTP, are part of the wider shift towards dispersed community governance described in this book; a shift that is unlikely to be reversible in the foreseeable future.

## Pain, banishment and exclusion

From New York (Kelling and Coles, 1996: 108) to Cleveland (Romeanes cited in Dean, 1997: 23) ZTP is unequivocally about 'taking back the streets'. However, this objective has different connotations in different places. By 1997, Middlesbrough, a town that had experienced severe long-term structural deprivation, faced the dubious distinction of having the cheapest heroin in Britain available on its streets. In effect, it was these accumulated social problems which provided the context for ZTP's emergence; initially, as a programme of 'rounding up the usual suspects' for purposes of information gathering; later as part of the transition towards a combined strategy of problem-oriented policing, crime reduction and community safety. In New York, the aims of ZTP were comparable to those in Middlesbrough: 'to regain control of public spaces' and to re-establish 'a modicum of civility and safety for ordinary citizens who travel daily along streets and by public transportation' (Kelling and Coles, 1996: 108–9). Yet, ZTP in New York was also different in significant respects. In order to illustrate this dissimilarity we must consider, once again, the issue of mass private spaces.

Mass private spaces – the gated communities, industrial parks, malls and recreational complexes within which people increasingly live, work, consume and play – are underpinned by contractual relations defining the rights and obligations of those who occupy them. These spaces constitute 'safe havens' for members and participants, a central technique in their management being to banish those who have no legitimate (contractual) right of entry. However, while banishment ensures safety for members during their occupancy of mass private space, it creates a problem. How do the occupants of mass private space safely negotiate the spatial interstices between 'safe havens' to which the excluded have been banished? In effect, 'safe havens' give rise to a 'conduit problem': how to ensure that people can move safely between fortified fragments? To date, three types of solutions have been directed at the conduit problem.

One solution has been to create private corridors between forti-fied fragments. One finds this solution in cities throughout North America in the form of walkways both above and below the ground. These walkways operate as extensions of mass private property by linking together the new feudal domains. Though such solutions are usually physical and situational, often drawing upon principles such as 'Crime Prevention Through Environmental Design', this is not always the case. For example, another important quasi-private form of conduit – whose efficacy is now called into question by the events of 11 September 2001 – has been provided by air travel.

A second solution has been for the private bodies, who wish to govern these interstitial spaces, to seek to do so themselves. In Cape Town residents and businesses routinely pay to have their public streets privately patrolled. The same pattern has occurred with the establishment of Business Improvement Districts (BIDs) in North America. In California, BIDs date back to the approval of Assembly Bill 103 ('The Parking and Business Improvement Area Law') in 1965. Today, California has approximately 200 BIDs. By the late 1990s 48 US states had passed laws enacting similar legislation and, at present, in New York City alone, there are no less than 41 BIDs. A BID is created when a group of business organisations joins together to take over responsibility for the promotion and improvement of the area, including the provision of services to supplement those that are already publicly provided. As exemplars of public–private partnership, BIDs often receive matched funding for their assessments from the city authorities. Security services are commonly included in the package of measures provided by BIDs. In Washington, 800 property owners in a 120-block downtown area raised $6 million per year to pay for 'tourist-friendly signs, additional street lighting, spruced-up paving, colourful banners . . . special machines for cleaning graffiti . . . [and uniformed] workers who patrol the district as combination unarmed security guards, information guides and goodwill ambassadors' (Puentes, 1997).

A third solution has been to focus the attention of professional (public) police on these interstitial areas so that they provide a policing service to meet the conduit policing requirements of gated communities. It is in this context that one has to understand the experience of ZTP in New York, the strategy being primarily (though not exclusively) a risk-based technique for policing the conduits between 'safe havens'. Considered in this light, ZTP marries together the banishment potential inherent in law enforcement and the traditional coercive capacities of police (sticks, handcuffs and guns) to engender a tactic that is dissimilar from traditional policing in two respects. First, by focusing on 'quality of life' offences rather than on major violations, it works on the assumption that 'paying attention to small problems in the present will prevent large ones in the future'. Second, in its application of physical coercion, the aim is no longer to alter the 'cost–benefit calculations' of rational actors but merely to employ pain for the purposes of banishment and exclusion. In effect, ZTP is a strategy for 'cleaning up the streets' by moving on risky people and, by so doing, engendering a situational consciousness in which risky persons and actions will no longer be tolerated. It comes as no surprise that one of the first places in which ZTP was initiated (we say 'one of the first places' because South Africa's apartheid pass laws also constituted a massive zero-tolerance strategy) was on the New York subway system. That system is a crucial conduit for people who occupy the many gated communities in and around New York City and for those who provide services to them. In New York the subway system constituted a risky place by virtue of having become a refuge for banished persons. William Bratton first initiated the policy of ZTP on the New York subway then brilliantly masterminded its extension to the conduits around Manhattan.

Our analysis of the experience of ZTP in these two locations would suggest both high levels of similarity and high levels of dissimilarity. In both Middlesbrough and New York ZTP was employed as a future-oriented, risk-based, intelligence-led strategy in which front-line officers used their lawful powers to 'take back the streets'. Yet, 'taking back the streets' had subtly different implications in the two locations. In Middlesbrough 'taking back the streets' had two meanings. On the one hand, police cracked down on acts of anti-social behaviour by young males (thereby aiming, in the words of Ray Mallon, to 'nip in the bud' future criminality) and took repeat property offenders out of circulation. On the other hand, officers used their legal powers not to arrest and charge, but to fuel a system of intelligence gathering, the (future-oriented) objective of which was to facilitate a long-term policy of crime reduction in an area of high structural deprivation. 'Taking back the streets' of New York undoubtedly involved a number of the same elements: the policing of quality of life offences, the systematic collection of street-level intelligence, the removal of repeat offenders from circulation and so on. Yet, New York was a very different place from Middlesbrough. Whereas the latter was plagued by long-term economic decline, the former contained significant tracts of mass private space surrounded by 'dangerous' areas. For that reason, a specific aim of ZTP in New York was to police the 'conduit problem'.

Before concluding this section it is worth reviewing our argument and adding a final observation. Though, as we have suggested in this section, the specific application of ZTP may vary somewhat from place to place, the strategy has a number of common features. First, ZTP is a risk-based, intelligence-led form of community policing. Second, it deploys traditional (coercive) means in the pursuit of non-traditional (preventive) ends. Third, it is linked to strategies of banishment and exclusion, though the precise character of these strategies may vary from place to place. (In New York banishment involved direct spatial exclusion; in Middlesbrough, an area lacking mass private spaces, it was also related to wider management of socially excluded populations.) Fourth, and most obviously, professional police undertake ZTP.

This final point deserves further consideration. Previously, we suggested that three solutions (the construction of 'private corridors', the creation of BIDs and the application of ZTP by professional public police) have been used to address the conduit problem. However, a fourth strategy – what might be called the deprofessionalisation of ZTP – has begun to emerge in Europe during the last decade. Essentially this development involves the use of citizens without police powers (sometimes employed directly by the municipal government and sometimes contracted by the municipality from outside organisations, such as commercial security companies) in policing quality of life offences such as fare-dodging, vandalism, public drunkenness and littering. During the 1980s municipal initiatives in the Netherlands were linked to the government's comprehensive plans for social crime prevention and included the involvement of occupational groups such as janitors, shop assistants, sports coaches and youth workers in 'the strengthening of non-police surveillance of possible law-breakers' in private, public and semi-public areas of life (Van Dijk and Junger-Tas, 1988: 264–5). In 1988 the Dutch government subsidised the appointment of 150 social caretakers in 130 public housing estates whose function was to deal with residents' problems and to undertake patrols in order to deter vandalism and petty crime. Soon after, a number of Dutch municipalities set up City Guard schemes, the function of uniformed Guards being to undertake preventive street patrols, to assist in the prevention of crime and nuisance and to provide public re-assurance.

In Britain similar provision also appeared in the 1980s when some local authorities established security forces, using funds from state employment initiatives. The first council-funded scheme proper was set up in Sedgefield, County Durham, in 1994. The main objectives of the Sedgefield Community Force are to increase public safety and re-assurance by the provision of foot and mobile patrols, to consult with local residents and the police on local problems of crime and anti-social behaviour, to provide advice and information to local residents about crime prevention and to observe and report offences to the police when they occur. This last point raises the issue of how the Community Force interacts with the local Durham constabulary. Here, a comment from Sedgefield Council's Customer Relations Officer is particularly pertinent, suggesting that the Community Force might have an extended role in policing those very quality of life offences hitherto undertaken by the professional police: 'The police have to focus on priorities that move away from minor criminal activity and nuisance. We believe that we are filling the gap' (cited in I'Anson and Wiles, 1995: 4).

More recently, state funding has been used to establish Neighbourhood Wardens schemes in various towns and cities throughout England and Wales. Wardens provide services that contribute to the aims of community safety as specified in the Crime and Disorder Act 1998. The core functions of wardens include crime prevention (assisting with the reduction of crime and more importantly the fear of crime), environmental improvement (helping in the improvement of the quality of life of residents) and community development (enhancing informal social control within local communities).

In research carried out on a scheme recently established by West Lancashire District Council in the North West of England (Johnston and Donaldson, forthcoming) community wardens were contracted by the council from a reputable private security company, and trained by the police in conjunction with council and company personnel, to provide uniformed foot patrols across the district. Several things may be noted about this scheme. First, wardens are involved in crime prevention and intelligence-gathering in conjunction with local police, a weekly meeting with the local police intelligence officer facilitating information exchange. Warden patrols may be asked to look out for named persons or vehicles and they are also given information on local crime 'hot spots'. Community wardens patrol on foot on a regular basis, being significantly more visible than the police, and there is evidence to suggest that some members of the public are more likely to pass on information to wardens than they are to police officers. Second, although the wardens initiative is part of a national community safety strategy, the aim of schemes is to provide – in partnership with other agencies – local solutions to local problems. To that extent, there are parallels between today's community wardens and the long-superseded borough police forces of days gone by. Officers in these forces were expected not just to engage in enforcement but also to be repositories of local knowledge for use in routine problem-solving, such as knowing which council department to telephone in order to have an abandoned car removed from local waste ground.

Third, wardens deal with a wide range of quality of life issues: from monitoring empty council properties, to arranging removal of litter from public spaces; and from making themselves visible at traffic 'hot spots' to engaging in surveillance of disruptive youths.

It is also significant that wardens in the West Lancashire scheme provided crucial evidence in the enforcement of the district's first Anti-Social Behaviour Order. Under the Anti-Social Behaviour Order provisions of the Crime and Disorder Act 1998, a local authority or a police authority may obtain a court order against an individual who engages in 'anti-social conduct' that causes or is likely to cause 'harassment, alarm or distress' to one or more people living in a different household from the defendant. An order can be made against anyone who is at least 10 years old directing him or her to refrain from engaging in the conduct involved, or from any other conduct described in the order. The order must run for at least two years and any violation of it without reasonable excuse is a criminal offence with a maximum penalty on indictment of five years in prison. In the particular case in question, an 18-year-old youth from Skelmersdale, West Lancashire, was served with a four-year order barring him from specified areas of the town after being accused of violent and aggressive behaviour, intimidation, vandalism and using foul and abusive racist language. Much of the evidence used to support this case was provided by community wardens who, at the time the research was undertaken, confidently expected the offender to breach the Order and anticipated that they would provide the evidence of such a breach.

Two observations may be made about these developments. First, for all their utility in addressing problems of nuisance, violence and racial harassment, an ethical issue has to be addressed. It has been noted that the legislation permits someone to be banished from a specified public or semi-public space on the basis of having committed non-criminal conduct deemed to be anti-social. Moreover, such exclusion need not remain conduct dependent since the person may be barred from re-entering the space even after desisting from the conduct which triggered the order in the first place (Von Hirsch and Shearing, 2000). Second, while the research in West Lancashire was being undertaken, the community wardens and the Anti-Social Behaviour Unit began to work from the same office. It would appear then, if West Lancashire is anything to go by, that non-professional personnel, lacking formal powers of enforcement, will play an increasingly important role in facilitating the banishment process.

## Conclusion

In this chapter we have considered ZTP in the context of two broad developments: the shift towards community governance and partnership; and the movement towards re-feudalisation through the development of mass private space. The second of these developments, in particular, raises normative questions about the degrees of accessibility that excluded and non-excluded groups may enjoy in the future in respect of security and justice. Many academic critics have argued that existing responses to these developments, such as ZTP, merely exacerbate inequality and inequity. While this may be true, it is also worth considering the possible benefits that may be associated with the various solutions discussed in this chapter. Here, several points are worthy of note. First, risk-based practices shift our focus from the past (and from preoccupation with retribution) to the present (and how best to promote the future). Second, community-based practices challenge police ownership of policing. One positive feature of William Bratton's early programme was to network police capacities with the capacities of other agencies, a development which became central to the Middlesbrough initiative. Third, community-based initiatives tend to localise control over security. This is evident in the contracts of governance that are associated with the new fortified spaces and which often, though not invariably, enable people to have influence over regulation of the places they inhabit. Paradoxically, one of the problems with ZTP when deployed for purposes of conduit policing, is that it fails to provide occupants of public space (street people) with any opportunity to influence policing in an equivalent way. In the final chapter we address the normative issues arising from these and other developments more fully. Before doing that, however, we review, once again, some of the key changes in security governance first outlined in Chapter 2. In order to do this we focus on Britain as an exemplar of 'the new security governance'.

# 7

# SECURITY GOVERNANCE
# IN BRITAIN

## Introduction

In Chapter 2 we outlined eight dimensions of governance which, together, provide a basis for understanding changes in the governance of security. We also pointed to the key role of mentalities in influencing those different dimensions. One important qualification was added to this analysis: that the changing dynamics of security governance do not involve a simple alignment between mentalities and their 'corresponding' dimensions. Instead, we argued that current trends in the governance of security display complexity at the empirical level, 'pure' forms of governance being the exception rather than the rule. In the present chapter we examine these issues further by focusing on a single example, recent developments in security governance in Britain. Our purpose in doing this is two-fold. On the one hand, Britain appears to provide an ideal location for exploring these changing governmental dynamics, particularly in the light of recent New Labour policies on criminal justice. On the other hand, consideration of British events also enables us to explore how the general trajectory of change outlined in Chapter 2 is undercut by complexity and empirical variation.

## Britain as an exemplar of the 'new security governance'

In Chapter 2 we discussed various dimensions of governance and noted several contemporary developments associated with them. When applied to the issue of security governance in Britain, a number of these developments are particularly noteworthy. In this section we consider five such developments.

## *State rule is no longer definitive*

Confirmation of this first development may be found at both trans-national and sub-national levels. In the former case, the growing influence of the European Union has provoked a debate in Britain about the impact of transnational governance on national state sovereignty. One perverse feature of this debate is that conservatives and radicals find themselves in partial agreement with one another. Conservatives claim that Britain's traditions and institutions are overridden by the whims of Brussels bureaucrats. Radicals allege that an 'authoritarian European state' is emerging whose practices are secretive and whose principal objective is to exclude Third World migrants from entry into Northern Europe (Bunyan, 1991). Though undoubtedly reflecting serious concerns about justice and accountability in matters of migration and human rights, however, such radical claims need to be treated with caution. The suggestion that transnational co-operation in policing and criminal justice constitutes proof of the existence of a European state (whether authoritarian or merely bureaucratic) is unconvincing. As Hebenton and Thomas suggest, the more there is bilateral and multi-lateral co-operation between European states over matters such as criminal justice, the more such arrangements will limit the autonomy of states. Far from producing a European 'super-state', the greater likelihood is a 'patchwork . . . of contexts, coalitions and interactions within and between national societies that escape the effective control of the central policy organs of government' (Hebenton and Thomas, 1995: 3).

Supranationalisation of the processes and institutions of formal government in Europe is one thing. There has also been an expansion of transnational corporate governance. This is most apparent in respect of global commercial security. In 1999 the Swedish-based company, Securitas, paid £230 million pounds for the acquisition of Pinkerton. The purchase gave rise to the world's largest security company, having combined sales of around £2 billion and employing 114,000 staff (a figure almost equivalent to the combined operational strength of all the police forces in England and Wales). Fifteen months later, the world's second largest security corporation was born when the Danish company Falk merged with one of the UK's largest security companies Group 4. Following the merger 'Group 4 Falk' had an annual turnover in excess of £1.25 billion and employed 115,000 staff. In March 2002, Group 4 Falk entered the North American security market through the acquisition of the

Wackenhut Corporation, the second largest provider of security services in the USA and Latin America. The combined enterprise will have 205,000 employees and a turnover of around $3.7 billion making it the largest security company in the world. Transnational commercial security companies undertake functions that were, hitherto, the prerogative of nation states. This is not only true in respect of prison privatisation where Britain has been a market leader and where British-based corporations, such as Securicor, have played a major role. (Securicor is now a major investor in private corrections in the USA.) Increasingly, major security companies define themselves in terms of their specialised *global* expertise. (Securicor's web page is headed by the message 'Global Expertise. Local Understanding'.) A good example is the London-based Control Risks Group that offers services in political and security risk analysis, confidential investigations, security consultancy and crisis management and response. Such companies undertake functions previously monopolised by states. In the early 1990s, for example, the South African company, Executive Outcomes, following an approach from a South American drugs enforcement agency, provided personnel to undertake 'Discretionary Warfare' (i.e. clandestine strikes) against drug-growers. The same company recently predicted with confidence that 'future peacekeeping/ refugee operations will be conducted more and more by companies like EO' (Executive Outcomes, 1998).

These developments are mirrored by those at the sub-national level. The Crime and Disorder Act 1998 is the most significant legislation in British criminal justice policy for a generation. The Act requires the police and local authorities – together with police authorities, health authorities and probation committees – to work together, in partnership with other agencies, to develop and implement a strategy for reducing crime and disorder in each district and unitary local authority area in England and Wales. A crucial principle behind the Act – the establishment of local community safety partnerships between public, commercial and voluntary bodies – reflects ongoing debates about the 'dispersal' and 're-invention' of government described in earlier chapters. This much is clear from Home Office Guidance on the Act. Partners, we are told, should avoid excessive preoccupation with structures, focusing instead on 'the goal of actually delivering safer communities'. Accordingly, the legislation 'does not prescribe in any detail what the agenda for the local partnership should be, nor what structures will be needed to deliver that agenda' (Home Office,

1999a). Local people, the Guidance insists, are best equipped to deal with these issues. For that reason the Act deliberately avoids attempting to define the terms 'crime' or 'disorder' on the grounds that the content of partner strategies must be driven by 'what matters to local people, and not constrained by artificial definitions imposed by central government'. The document also lists those bodies that must be asked to co-operate in partnerships. These include, among others: Neighbourhood Watch; Victim Support; shopkeepers, retail organisations and other employers; co-operatives and partnerships; trade unions; residents groups; religious groups; groups established in furtherance of good race relations; and groups established in the interests of women, young people, elderly people, the disabled, lesbians and gay men. Significantly, there is no assumption that some partners are 'more equal' than others:

> There should be no automatic assumption that the police and/or local authority will 'lead' every aspect of the work of the partnership at local level. Decisions should be approached on the basis that leadership will fall to whoever is best placed to provide it in the light of local circumstances and the nature of the specific issue.
>
> (Home Office, 1999a)

Finally, it is argued that the Key National Objectives which the Home Secretary sets for the police service will develop to reflect the increased emphasis which the Act places on local action and on preventing crime, rather than reacting to it. To that extent the local crime audits that reveal the 'reality of crime and disorder' in particular areas will have a direct impact on national policing policy.

To sum up. Transnational and sub-national developments, such as these, are by no means indicative of the demise of the nation state. Thus, it would be naïve to accept the agenda of 'dispersed governance', contained within New Labour's crime and disorder legislation, at face value. On the contrary, that agenda co-exists with various centralising tendencies, the effects of which are complex and unpredictable. As Crawford (2001) argues, network and partnership arrangements require 'hands off' forms of management which may be undermined by interventionist practices on the part of government. The result may be to produce forms of governance which are simultaneously 'at arm's length and hands on' (ibid.: 64). Yet, for all their complexity, the developments described here do confirm the emergence of a new morphology of governance in which state rule is no longer exclusive or definitive.

## Public and private interests overlap

Though, for reasons stated in Chapter 4, we reject the interest-based conception of governance, interests are commonly invoked as a means of explaining governing practices. In Chapter 2 we noted that the traditional distinction between 'public interests' and 'private interests' that is deployed in governing discourse becomes less clear-cut the more governance is dispersed. This is particularly evident in respect of conflicts associated with the various 'private orders' arising with mass private property (Shearing and Stenning, 1981, 1987) or with the development of 'gated communities' such as those in North America (Blakely and Snyder, 1997) and Britain (Tims, 2000). Similar issues arise in respect of CCTV surveillance in public places. Here (Von Hirsch, 2000) notes that two sets of issues arise. What legitimate rights of privacy or anonymity should people enjoy in public places, and how far does CCTV impinge on these rights? How far does the public goal of crime prevention legitimise such rights of privacy and anonymity being compromised?

Three distinct, but related, issues are at stake in respect of discursive debates about public and private interests. First, as in the CCTV example, there are normative disputes about the balance which needs to be struck between public and private interests. Second, there are questions about the constitution of different types of interests. A good example concerns the invocation of 'community' as a locus of public interests. The Crime and Disorder Act 1988 is predicated upon 'community safety' becoming an achievable governmental objective at the local level. Yet, the involvement of multiple partners in the formulation of community safety strategies may, paradoxically, increase the potential for plural conflicts of interest to emerge. This is particularly so since, in the current period, it is more realistic to perceive community as a locus of multiple and competing risks than as an expression of collective (public) interests (Johnston, 1997b). The dilemma for the legislation is whether partners will be able to respond to local sectional demands without undermining 'the public interest'. Third, there is the impact of changing governing practices on the distinction between public and private interests. Take the case of exclusionary strategies designed to keep those considered socially undesirable, or at risk of being undesirable in the future, from entering public places

(Von Hirsch, 2000). In this case, a risk-based practice is deployed, not only against those convicted of wrongdoing, but also against those who might commit future harms. In effect, an exclusionary practice is legitimised through the temporal re-configuration of interests: private interest being conceived as present and immediate; public interests as having a future, as well as a present, orientation.

### The governance of security becomes more future oriented

Previously we noted that all strategies of governance involve some combination of past and future orientations. The governance of security by state authorities has tended to be oriented to past events, partly because of its desire not to interfere with the constitutional rights of citizens. Corporate authorities, being free of such formal constraints, have been more preoccupied with governing the future. The Crime and Disorder legislation is founded, in considerable part, on the application of a future-oriented mentality to matters of crime and community safety. A rigorous exposition of that future-oriented mentality – and its relationship to the governance of the past in matters of criminal justice policy – can be found in a recent paper by the Home Office criminologist, Paul Ekblom. In this paper, Ekblom, drawing upon aspects of situational crime prevention and routine activities theory, explores, among other things, the temporal dimension of criminal policy. First and foremost, he argues, 'crime prevention focuses on the future' (Ekblom, 1998). The causes of crime are many and complex, some of them being remote. Yet, such remote influences ultimately work through immediate precursors that combine to generate the criminal event. Such precursors include 'offender . . . situation . . . target . . . favourable environment and . . . the absence of capable preventers' (ibid.). In Ekblom's view, then, the objective of crime prevention is to undermine this conjunction of factors: ' to . . . disrupt the conjunction of criminal opportunity, either by changing the situational or offender-related precursors in advance of the criminal event, or by preventing them coming together' (ibid.).

This account of crime prevention is expressed through the discourse of risk management.

> The preventive process is a way of forestalling future crime by identifying risks on the basis of past patterns of offending. *Anticipatory prevention* tracks new *emerging crime problems* and new *potential offenders* – the latter

through *audits of risk and protective factors* . . . It also scans further ahead to unfolding trends.

(ibid.: emphasis in original)

In Ekblom's view, one of the aims of this approach is to re-examine the relationship between 'the past' and 'the future' in matters of security governance: to consider how reactions to past crimes might prevent future ones; how the anticipation of future sanctions might deter today's offenders; or how intervention in present crimes might prevent future ones.

### The enhanced role of lay and commercial agents in security governance

It is also the case that commercial and lay personnel play an increasingly significant role in the execution of security governance. As Ekblom puts it: 'the professional's role is to *act at a distance* – to motivate, inform and assist other, often informal, preventers (such as families, teachers or site managers)' (ibid.: emphasis in original). This principle can be illustrated by three examples. First, in Britain as in other jurisdictions, there is a growing interest in restorative justice, elements of which may be seen in the Crime and Disorder Act 1998 and in the Youth Justice and Criminal Evidence Act 1999. A number of agencies are now experimenting with Family Group Conferences. This initiative was first developed in New Zealand under the Children, Young Persons and their Families Act 1989. In Britain the approach has been applied largely within the field of child welfare, though several attempts – notably in Thames Valley and Hampshire – have been made to employ the same principles to youth justice. Broadly speaking, this approach is associated with the practices of apology and forgiveness found in some indigenous cultures and given theoretical substance in Braithwaite's (1989) model of re-integrative shaming. Such re-integrative approaches assume the development of partnerships between criminal justice professionals and lay persons such as victims, offenders, their families and non-expert intermediaries.

A second example concerns the development of community-based supports aimed at reducing the risks posed by convicted sex offenders. 'Circles of Support and Accountability' were first developed by the Mennonite Central Committee in Ontario. Circles, which usually consist of between four and six people, draw up a members' covenant outlining their mutual expectations and what happens if they are broken. The core member (the offender) must state that he is committed to 'no more victims of sex abuse'. The initiative has now been developed at Wolvercote Clinic in the South of England where the Clinic Manager, Donald Findlater, has insisted that volunteers need life-skills rather than professional social work or counselling experience:

> We wanted people who had a life, and were willing to share that life. It helps if they are wise and a bit cautious, people with their feet on the ground, not too prurient, and not easily shocked. It's not a mind-delving exercise. It's befriending . . . it's . . . about doing things together . . . Sometimes this creates community that the core member may never have had before.
>
> (cited in Harthill, 2001: 5)

The same principle of lay involvement applies to neighbourhood (or community) wardens. Schemes of this sort have been in operation in Britain since the 1980s, though current governmental interest in them is, partly, the result of successful experiments in the Netherlands. A recent report – significantly produced under the auspices of the Social Exclusion Unit's 'Neighbourhood Renewal Initiative' – committed the government to setting up a new inter-departmental 'Neighbourhood Warden's Unit' to support the development of schemes (Social Exclusion Unit, 2000). The report sees neighbourhood wardens as contributing to security in its broadest sense. Of the fifty existing community schemes examined by the report's writers, a variety of security functions were regularly fulfilled: crime prevention; environmental improvement; housing management; community development; the provision of visits to vulnerable people such as tenants or intimidated victims; the collection and transmission of information to the police; and the provision of response to minor incidents of anti-social behaviour, including low-level neighborhood disputes. These tasks were found to be undertaken by a variety of personnel including neighbourhood patrols, concierges, caretakers and neighbourhood support workers.

Three points are worthy of note in respect of these schemes. First, several authors have noted the extent to which police organisations are now, increasingly, information-based (Ericson and Haggerty, 1997; Johnston, 2000a). The report places considerable emphasis upon the need for security partners to compile, collect and disseminate information.

Agencies involved in running/managing a neighbourhood warden scheme need to have systems in place for sharing information . . . good communications [are] . . . exhibited in a number of ways . . . knowing where to go for information you need but don't yourself have . . . having the ability to relay information quickly when an incident arises. One way of achieving this exchange of information is by drawing up a protocol with the police, local authorities and other partners.

(Social Exclusion Unit, 2000)

Second, the report notes that the involvement of suitably regulated private security companies in schemes can be legitimate, effective and efficient. Here, the report describes an effective and well-managed scheme run on the Aylesbury Estate. In this case, the local authority employed a commercial security firm to carry out uniformed patrols of the Estate's 2,200 properties in 1994. Subsequently, the scheme has grown to cover a further 4,515 properties. The contract is put out to tender each year and, to date three different companies have been employed. One of the conditions of the contract is that while the company providing the service may change, the same wardens are employed in order to ensure continuity of provision.

Third, the report places considerable emphasis on the role of neighbourhood wardens in fighting social exclusion and facilitating community renewal. Particular importance is given to the involvement in and the recruitment of ethnic minorities, the old, the young and the disabled to such schemes. To that extent, the neighbourhood wardens initiative is concerned not only with the development of security networks, but with the development of security networks which are representative of the communities to which they are accountable.

### Security governance becomes both more 'distanciated' and more 'embedded'

Earlier we made reference to the fact that security governance is more 'distanciated' than hitherto. The example to which we have just referred – the deployment of lay and commercial personnel in the formation of local security networks ('partnerships') – is a good example of such distanciation. The British government, like others adopting a neo-liberal mentality, devolves more and more responsibility for the execution of security to communities themselves. One obvious way of doing this is by a process of territorial dispersal: devolving tasks to the 'local communities' and 'neighbourhoods' described in the Social Exclusion Unit report. An alternative mechanism is the 'functional dispersal' of security responsibilities. In this case, security governance may become a function, or part-function, of human agents or physical objects. As to the first, many people working in commercial organisations now find that they have security obligations embedded (either formally or informally) in their work roles. Consider an example from a field known to both of us. In Britain, as elsewhere, the impact of New Public Management in universities has meant that academic staff now bear responsibility not just for academic quality but also for the corporate assets attached to it. The supervision of research students now involves detailed record keeping (dated and signed copies to all parties) outlining what was discussed in meetings and what was agreed. The purpose of this exercise is not only to facilitate student progress, but also to ensure that the institution may be protected from the risk of litigation posed by dissatisfied consumers. As to the second, for twenty years the Home Office has been a leading instigator of situational models of crime prevention, the object of which is to reduce criminal opportunities through the manipulation of physical space (e.g. by 'designing out crime' or protecting 'defensible space'). As a mode of (physically embedded) security governance, CCTV is both backward-looking (recording past events) and forward-looking (predicting events to come). In this latter regard, two British scientists have recently developed a software package which they claim is able to predict deviant behaviour – such as car theft – by matching the movements of those on film with a library of normal and pathological gaits.

> The new technology . . . matches up the outlines of . . . objects with a library of movements to anticipate when a crime could occur, [since] thieves tend to approach vehicles in a different way from their rightful owners . . . There are also plans to use this technology in London Underground stations to identify suicide risks from passengers who jump in front of trains.
>
> (*Computer Active*, 2000: 10)

## From the exemplary to the empirical

### *Mentalities and techniques of justice*

The picture we have painted above is by no means an inaccurate one. However, as we have insisted, there is no simple alignment between governing mentalities and their 'corresponding' techniques. Consider the example of CCTV, previously discussed. At one time, the use of CCTV was restricted to private places (such as factories and offices) or to public–private ones (such as shopping malls). In these cases, governance was achieved through the compliance of those who occupied the spaces in question. Workers might be required to subject themselves to visual surveillance as a condition of their wage labour contracts. Those wishing to shop in malls might be required to undergo it as a precondition of entry to them. Latterly, the unprecedented transfer of visual surveillance from private (or public–private) places to public streets has apparently demonstrated the willingness of British citizens to comply with the authorities' use of routine surveillance.

It would be wrong to conclude, however, that the actuarial mentality underpinning the police's use of visual security necessarily restricts the range of techniques they employ. Though visual surveillance is, primarily, focused on the minimisation of risk and harm, police continue to use coercive and enforcement-based techniques alongside it. In recent years there has been much controversy about the British police's tracking and high-speed pursuit of stolen vehicles – a practice now invariably aided by aerial surveillance cameras. Following the deaths of several people hit by speeding pursuit cars, critics castigate the police for their adoption of an enforcement-led strategy, rather than the harm-minimising one that a surveillance-based approach might imply. We should not be surprised by this paradox. After all, the previous chapter demonstrated that ZTP, far from being reducible to a single mentality, bears a complex relationship to the varied technologies of community policing. That the empirical relationship between mentalities and techniques is a complex one may be illustrated further by considering some aspects of British criminal justice policy.

While punishment has a pivotal role in British criminal justice, other paradigms have been, and remain, influential. One of these ('welfare') was particularly significant until the late 1970s. Others such as 'risk management' and 'restoration' have grown in influence over the last twenty years. The interaction of these later influences with the earlier ones has begun to re-shape criminal justice in Britain. Yet, being subject to the effects of various mediating factors, that process is neither linear nor uniform. Consider, for example, the influence of party politics. Downes and Morgan (1997) identified three stages in the post-war politics of law and order. During the first of these, which lasted until 1970, a non-partisan consensus prevailed with most parties subscribing to a broadly 'liberal-progressive' criminal justice ideology. Significantly, however, this ideology was not shared by the judiciary who continued to adopt retributive-deterrent principles of sentencing. The second phase, whose consolidation was made complete by the Thatcher election victory of 1979, was the era of 'partisan law and order' politics. During this time the retributive approach of the Conservatives established hegemony over Labour's spasmodic efforts to link crime to unemployment and inequality. In the 1990s a third phase developed in which Conservative governments combined populist penal measures with the application of neo-liberal economic policies to criminal justice. During this period a new populist consensus was adopted by both major parties, the similarities between them suggesting that, for the foreseeable future, law and order politics would remain 'the politics of the "hard centre"' (Johnston, 1997a). Such was the force of this populism that Labour, prior to the 1997 election victory, attempted to 'out-tough' the Conservatives on criminal justice issues. Since its election the Labour government has tried to balance this obligation to 'toughness' with its commitment to crime prevention, victim support and community safety.

Of course, this recent shift between emphases is part of a longer historical picture. For more than a century British criminal justice policy was the product of a dialogue between punishment and welfare models, slippage between these models moving policy sometimes one way ('more punishment'), sometimes the other ('more welfare'). From 1945 until 1970 a welfare-oriented consensus dominated official thinking. A decade later that official consensus was destroyed by the incoming Conservative government's commitment to punishment, Labour retaining a residual attachment to welfare. Yet, this image of competition between dual paradigms is, itself, too simplistic. The parsimony of the punishment model – its explanatory neatness, its appeal to popular sentiments, and its ease of deployment in political discourse – has always enabled it to shape key features of the justice agenda even when the welfare model has been in relative ascendancy. Moreover, in recent times, the disintegration of the welfare paradigm has coincided with the emergence of alternative mentalities oriented around concepts of risk and restoration. The result has been a criminal justice system oriented around four broad mentalities (Table 3).

- *Punishment* proposes state infliction of penal sanctions on individual offenders, in order to incapacitate, to right wrongs and to provide a symbolic re-affirmation of the status quo.
- *Welfare* proposes that criminal justice professionals reform offenders through their 'normalisation', taking into account the social conditions of offending behaviour and having, as an objective, the re-inclusion of offenders into society.
- *Risk* involves the adoption (by corporate, state or voluntary agents) of instrumental techniques for the management and minimisation of risk, and the application of such techniques to those deemed to constitute potential sources of risk.
- *Restoration* involves the adoption by multiple agents – including community and lay agents – of problem-oriented techniques for repairing relations between offenders and victims, and for facilitating the achievement of outcomes considered 'just' by the different parties.

*Table 3* Four models of criminal justice

|  | Punishment | Welfare | Risk | Restoration |
|---|---|---|---|---|
| *Object of intervention* | Offender (as individual) | Offender (in society) | Offenders, victims, offences, locations, and other risk factors | Offenders and victims |
| *Agent of intervention* | State/ professional | State/ professional | Multiple agents/ knowledges | Multiple agents/ importance of lay knowledge |
| *Aims* | Penalisation | Normalisation | Minimisation | Reparation/ integration |
| *Rationality* | Symbolic ('tough on crime') | Reformist ('tough on the causes of crime') | Instrumental | Problem-oriented |
| *Method* | Incapacitation/ exclusion | Care/ inclusion | Surveillance/ management | Communication/ resolution |

## Empirical complexity

These four mentalities are by no means mutually exclusive. On the contrary, there is both overlap and interaction between them, their combination and re-combination producing an empirical reality that is both complex and unpredictable. Some of the features of that complexity may be demonstrated by considering a single example.

In the early 1980s the punishment-oriented Thatcher government instituted the 'short, sharp shock' in detention centres for young offenders. The experiment – which involved inmates partaking in substantial amounts of physical exercise and military drill within highly disciplined regimes – proved unsuccessful in reducing rates of recidivism and was soon abandoned. By the mid-1980s it was clear that both the police (who were increasingly using powers of cautioning) and the juvenile courts (which were using custodial sentences less frequently) were veering towards welfare-oriented principles of minimum intervention in the lives of young offenders. At the same time, as Rutherford (1996) notes, key figures in the Home Office began to recognise that the same minimalist principles could be applied more widely to the justice system. Consequently, the government became increasingly committed to community sanctions, rather than to custodial ones, on the grounds of both effectiveness and cost. Such a policy had major implications for the probation service. As David Faulkner, the senior official responsible for criminal justice policy put it in 1989 'transformation from a social work agency to a criminal justice agency with a social work base must be completed if the service is to do what is now expected of it' (cited in Rutherford, 1996: 107–8).

The groundwork for transformation was, in fact, already being put into place. In 1984 a Statement of National Objectives for probation had been formulated, part of whose purpose was to subject the service to the strictures of 'new public management'. This drive towards greater effectiveness, efficiency and value for money was to be combined with a re-definition of the service's core philosophy. Historically, the role of probation (significantly defined in the 1967 Probation Act as the 'probation and after care service') had been to 'advise, assist and befriend' its clients. This welfare model of probation practice was, however, to be given a new twist after the 1991 Criminal Justice Act with the service's key function now being defined as the administration of 'punishment in the community'. From here on probation orders ceased to be defined as 'alternatives to custody', becoming punishments in their own right.

This conflation of punishment, welfare and managerial models within the Thatcher administration – a product of the tension between neo-liberalism and neo-Conservatism – was to be complicated by a further development. The 1991 Act had also emphasised the probation service's role in the protection of the public. Towards that end the Association of Chief Officers of Probation issued a position statement on the management of risk and public protection which called for a 'cultural shift' in the work of the service towards more active recognition of its responsibility in managing risk. The resulting guidance recommended that risk assessment (with regular review) be carried out in all cases, that interagency working and the design of protocols for information exchange be put into place, and that common computerised and integrated recording systems be implemented. In short, probation was defined as one agency within an integrated governmental complex oriented towards the management of security risks (compare Ericson and Haggerty, 1997).

This interaction between punishment, welfare and risk-based models continues to be reflected in youth justice policy. A year before its 1997 election victory New Labour published plans for the reform of the youth justice system (Labour Party, 1996) which included reform of the cautioning system, speeding up the youth justice system for persistent offenders, initiating new court orders and introducing new multi-agency Youth Justice Teams. These proposals were eventually included in the Crime and Disorder Act 1998. Labour's approach to youth justice had to be seen as part of its wider commitment to being 'tough on crime, tough on the causes of crime'. This slogan is interesting because as well as being a key element in the Party's attempt to 'out-tough' the Conservatives on law and order matters prior to the 1997 election, it also demonstrated Labour's commitment to a cocktail of control mechanisms: punishment ('tough on crime'), welfare ('tough on the causes of crime'), risk minimisation and restorative justice.

The effect is a complicated one. On the one hand, the legislation puts emphasis on restorative justice whereby young offenders can be called upon to make reparation, either to specific individuals, or to the wider community. On the other hand, it links the values of punishment and welfare in an uneasy combination. One recurrent theme is that adults accept their parental responsibilities. Yet, critics have noted the tension between Labour's desire to punish the irresponsible and their wider commitment to policies of social inclusion. Thus, Newburn asks, while there is considerable evidence that poor parenting and inconsistent parental discipline are key risk factors in offending, is it really appropriate that they be dealt with through court orders and coerced attendance at parenting classes? Equally, should youthful 'anti-social behaviour' be tackled by the introduction of curfews and other processes that bring younger and younger children within the ambit of the criminal justice system? (Newburn, 1998).

In the light of this empirical complexity, it is interesting to consider recent debates about the nomenclature of the 'probation' service. In 1998 the Home Office published a discussion paper, *Joining Forces to Protect the Public* (Home Office, 1998), which set out Government plans for effective joint work between the prison and probation services. The document noted that existing legislation, directing probation officers to 'advise, assist and befriend' their clients, was now 'completely out of line' with the everyday reality of probation practice. Further, it suggested, since the service 'recognises that its core function is public protection', the statutory role of probation officers should be amended to emphasise both their need to 'confront, challenge and change offending behaviour' and to 'recognise punishment as a central part of that process'. By these means, it was argued, the public will come to understand and value more highly the work that probation staff do on their behalf.

The document went on to stress that the title used by the service should reflect, accurately, its aims and objectives. Existing terms, it was suggested, might convey inappropriate messages: 'probation' might be seen as a conditional reprieve and, as such, tolerant of crime; 'community service' might be interpreted, incorrectly, as a mere 'voluntary' activity. Though the government had 'no strong preference on the potential name for a new unified national Probation Service' it insisted that the one chosen should be 'capable of inspiring public confidence in the work of that Service'. Accordingly, the document listed several possible names for debate:

- the Public Protection Service
- the Community Justice Enforcement Agency
- the Community Sentence Enforcement Service
- the Justice Enforcement and Public Protection Service
- the Public Safety and Offender Management Service
- the Community Protection and Justice Service.

Following discussion, the government proposed that the new unified national service would be called the 'Community Punishment and

Rehabilitation Service'. This juxtaposition of two penal mentalities was an attempt to mediate between those who had favoured a 'community justice' orientation and those who had favoured a 'community punishment' one. In the event, major opposition to the proposal from Members of Parliament, who had been lobbied successfully by criminal justice professionals, led to the title being dropped. In March 1999 the Criminal Justice and Courts Services Bill was published, the new integrated service being given the compromise title 'The National Probation Service for England and Wales'. Whether this new title will be capable of inspiring public confidence in the work of the service in the manner desired by government is open to question. What is unarguable, however, is that its blandness facilitates the combination and re-combination of punishment, rehabilitation, risk and restoration in ever more complex forms.

It also remains to be seen where these developments move probation. Nash (1999a, 1999b, 2000), who has written extensively about the impact of risk and dangerousness on the re-configuration of the probation service in England and Wales, draws a pessimistic conclusion. In his view probation functions are being subsumed beneath the police's goals of 'surveillance, control and exclusion': 'This points much more to a policy aimed at managing the problem (and therefore managing the risk) than working at longer-term strategies aimed at reducing the risk' (Nash, 2000: 211). In particular, he suggests, the prevention of crimes by 'low risk' offenders is now of little consequence to a newly constituted probation service preoccupied with managing more serious ones. Whether or not this pessimistic conclusion is justified depends, of course, on political considerations. It is to such considerations that we now turn.

## Penal volatility and beyond

The previous discussion suggests that British penal policy is in a volatile state. Yet, such volatility is not peculiar to Britain. Referring to the wider picture, Rose has recently drawn attention to the

> bewildering variety of developments in regimes of control
> . . . from demands for execution or preventive detention
> of implacably dangerous or risky individuals . . . to the
> development of dispersed, designed in-control regimes for
> the continual, silent and largely invisible work of the

assessment, management, communication and control
of risk.

(2000: 321)

Control regimes have fluctuated dramatically during recent years:
from 'nothing works' to 'prison works'; from community sanctions
to 'boot camps'; from re-integration to 'three strikes and you're
out'; and from incapacitation to reparation. As Rose suggests,
'there appears to be little strategic coherence about these developments at the level of their rationalities, and much diversity and
contingency at the level of their technologies' (ibid.: 321). Indeed, as
our review of British events suggest, the position is even more complicated: 'not only because in most jurisdictions several inconsistent
penological regimes or forms are in place, but also because in some
jurisdictions virtually all may be available as options' (O'Malley,
1999: 176). Two issues arise with respect to penal volatility. First,
how do we explain it? Second, what are its future prospects?

Three influential analyses of contemporary governance have been
employed to explain penal volatility (ibid.). While recognising their
general importance in the field of governance theory, however,
O'Malley claims that each has specific limitations in explaining
such volatility. Garland's (1996) claim that dual policy shifts
(between 'responsibilisation' and punishment) reflect the 'limits of
the sovereign state', ignores a complex of possible alternatives.
Simon's (1995) claim that 'nostalgic' penal practices (such as 'boot
camps' and 'community policing') reflect an emerging 'postmodernity', fails to capture developments which are either
innovative (e.g. prisoner enterprise schemes) or which display both
nostalgic and innovative elements (e.g. partnership – rather than
'social contract' – models of community policing). However, it is
the third account – the explanation of volatility in terms of the
impact of neo-liberal political rationality – that is most relevant to
the present discussion. In this case, volatility is explained by neo-
liberalism's integration of several diverse concerns: the desire to
shrink state governance; the wish to challenge welfare dependency;
the advocacy of the market as a model of governance; the desire for
effectiveness, efficiency and accountability in service delivery; the
re-affirmation of personal, familial and community responsibility;
and the invocation of freedom of choice over other values.

Ostensibly, neo-liberalism can provide a convincing account of
penal volatility. For example, restitution may be said to define the
victim as a customer, to make the offender personally responsible

for his or her actions, to remove the state from governance and to promote, in its place, quasi-market-like relations. Likewise, incapacitation might be said to reflect the neo-liberal urge for accountability since it produces cost-effective solutions, prioritises the needs of victim-consumers and holds offenders personally responsible for their actions. However, O'Malley rightly questions whether the same political rationality can genuinely account for the rise of boot camps *and* incapacitation *and* re-integration *and* prisoner enterprise schemes, particularly when it fails to 'confront the contradictory nature of the diverse formulations and practices of penal policy that are presented as consistent with this rationality' (O'Malley, 1999: 184).

Neo-liberal analysis has tended to regard the penal variations arising under conservative regimes – and latterly under social democratic ones – as the reflection of a single political rationality. Yet, in reality, such volatility is the product of at least two interacting rationalities: neo-liberalism and neo-conservatism (ibid.). This point is particularly crucial to an understanding of the British experience during the last decade. Previously – in a discussion of developments in British policing during the 1980s – one of us emphasised the importance of differentiating between the constituent elements of the Thatcherite 'New Right':

> 'Toryism' . . . encapsulates both the values of authority (of the state over its subjects) and of responsibility (of the state to its subjects) . . . Whereas 'Tories' regard their values as socially integrative . . . modern 'Conservatism' has come to be associated with the particular interests and values of the business class. During recent years . . . Conservatives have . . . become more and more committed to 'neo-liberal' ideology, the view that individual liberties are best secured by the 'invisible hand' of the market.
>
> (Johnston, 1992a: 2)

In that analysis it was argued that elements of both rationalities ('free economy' and 'strong state') had produced volatile police policy (including nationalisation of public order policing *and* growing privatisation *and* the growth of 'active citizenship'). It was also suggested that future policy would be a product, not just of the juxtaposition of those competing rationalities, but of their growing interpenetration. O'Malley's analysis captures precisely how that interpenetration has impacted on penal policy:

. . . penal policies over the past two decades have been formed by regimes that amalgamate and combine rather contradictory governing rationalities. Unity between them is possible, [such as in their] shared hostility to regimes of the welfare-interventionist state. However, these and many other points of overlap . . . disguise quite distinct and often contradictory positions.

(1999: 188)

What implications for the future governance of security can be drawn from this analysis? First and foremost, we would argue, if volatility in criminal justice is the product, not just of neo-liberalism, but also of a 'heterogeneous alliance' between neo-liberal and neo-conservative rationalities (O'Malley, 1999: 190), or the even more fractured set of mentalities we outlined earlier, consideration has to be given to the political conditions which mediate between governing rationalities and their 'outcomes'. To put it another way, 'outcomes' cannot be conceived as the 'product' of singular governing rationalities. This much was confirmed by our discussion of the British experience where it was shown that rationalities are often inconsistent; that they are subject to combination and re-combination; that there is no simple correlation between them and their 'associated' technologies; and that they are affected by political conditions.

An important issue arises from this. If there is no one-to-one relationship between rationalities and 'outcomes', might the same rationalities, under different political conditions, support different normative programmes and facilitate different substantive outcomes? In commenting on this O'Malley (1997: 378) refers to 'possibilities for disaggregating neo-liberal strategies and practices, and rendering their often highly innovative developments available for appropriation in a "progressive" post-welfare politics' (see also Shearing, 1995; compare also Foucault, 1991; Burchell, 1993). So far, analysis of the impact of risk-based thinking has focused on its limitations and dangers: its capacity to support invasive systems of surveillance and control; its tendency to support 'actuarial' rather than 'real' modes of justice; and its use, in combination with coercive forms of control, to penalise powerless minorities (Simon, 1988; Feeley and Simon, 1994; Hudson, 1996). Though these issues are vitally important, they are predicated upon two questionable assumptions: that risk is invariably used to support the ends of coercion and control; and that, irrespective of the political conditions surrounding their deployment, risk-based techniques inevitably produce pathological effects. In the following chapter we dispense with these assumptions and consider, instead, whether an alternative normative framework can be married to the mentality of risk.

# 8

# NODAL GOVERNANCE, SECURITY AND JUSTICE

## Introduction

In this chapter we explore one possible basis for integrating the governance of security and justice and suggest that the model of 'nodal governance' provides a useful framework within which to situate normative questions about the governance of security. In pursuing our argument we need, first, to re-visit a few of the main points identified previously. Earlier in the book we outlined the various concepts ('mentalities', 'institutions', 'technologies' and 'practices') that we proposed to employ in the analysis of security governance. One implication of our adoption of this conceptual framework was to affirm that, far from being natural or pre-ordained, different modalities of security governance are the product of different applications of human invention. Regimes of security governance are a product of the mentalities that people have applied in the past and of those that they might apply in the future. Critically, this analytical approach exposes the normative basis of security governance: the fact that security programmes and practices, far from being merely technical discourses, carry underlying normative considerations, the implications of which have to be borne by their inventors.

While emphasising that mentalities are a vital element in the creation and re-creation of security paradigms and in the technologies, institutions and practices through which they are enacted, we also stressed that the approach taken here was a 'governance-based', rather than an 'interest-based' one. In Chapters 2 and 4 we outlined some of the problems arising from the interest-based approach, two of which are particularly problematic: its tendency to see peoples' objectives as 'given' by social interests rather than as the product of complex discursive processes; and its tendency to assume a correspondence between those objectives and the outcomes they seek to enact. We suggested in Chapter 4 that the Anglo-American model of police history exemplifies both of these tendencies, regarding the institutions and practices of the 'new police' as a product of the 'unfolding' of given 'interests'. By contrast we have argued that the relationship between governing mentalities, and the institutions, technologies and practices associated with them is an 'enabling', rather than a 'determining' one. Those committed to particular governing mentalities will undoubtedly utilise the institutional, technical and practical conditions that they believe will best enable their enactment, but there can be no guarantee that those conditions have the capacity to secure the objectives with which they are aligned. On the contrary, our discussion of security governance in Britain (Chapter 7) demonstrated the extent to which technological and institutional conditions may be undercut by a variety of political factors that mediate between mentalities, their objectives and their outcomes.

The refusal to posit a simple correspondence between governing mentalities, the conditions of their enactment and the outcomes towards which they are directed raises two issues. First, it suggests the need to situate debates about security governance within a strategic framework and having done so, to pose salient political and normative questions: for example, which political alliances, local conditions and agency configurations are most likely to facilitate the achievement of desired security objectives under any given set of conditions? Second, such strategic thinking needs, also, to be realistic about the limits and possibilities of change. In the second section of this chapter we shall outline a proposal for integrating security and justice that draws upon a risk-based approach. Notwithstanding our commitment to this model, it would be strategically naïve to assume that its enactment would eradicate, for all time, the influence of the punishment paradigm. Indeed, we have observed in previous chapters how the punishment model places limits on the efficacy of the alternative practices with which it co-exists. Similarly, it would be naïve to assume that the approach we propose is equally valid to all circumstances. On the contrary, while the general principles that underpin the approach are central to our argument, we recognise that the strategic application of those principles will vary according to conditions. We also recognise that there are other possibilities, other than the risk-based one we will review, for integrating the doing of justice and security. For example, one of us has recently explored the possibilities for such an integration presented by 'restorative justice' (Shearing, 2001).

We also suggested that analysis of the day-to-day reality of security regimes, rather than of their mentalities and enabling conditions alone, confirm the contingent and variable nature of security. This may be evidenced in a number of different ways. For example, in Chapter 1 we pointed out that security depends upon more than the presence or absence of given material conditions. On the contrary, people's experience of security will be the product of 'comfort thresholds' that are themselves affected by the interaction of various objective threats and subjective experiences. Crucially, security is also affected by local conditions. In the same chapter we drew attention to the example of young people on 'Willowdene' whose security was inextricably linked to local knowledge networks and to routine, everyday practices. Later in this chapter we suggest that the mobilisation of local knowledge is fundamental to the construction of just and democratic forms of security governance.

At the outset of this book we also spoke of the need to balance security with alternative values such as liberty, privacy and justice. A particularly critical issue in this regard concerns the relative balance that should obtain between security and justice. We have argued that while tensions may exist between the two, such is their mutual interdependence that authorities wishing to govern security more effectively should pursue justice more diligently. In the past, the punishment model offered a parsimonious means – albeit, as we have demonstrated in previous chapters, a flawed means – for integrating security and justice. In the present, a more complicated alignment of security and justice is evident. We argued in Chapter 5 that the paradigm of risk – at least insofar as it is applied through the 'actuarial' model of justice – decouples justice from security, re-integrates them in new combinations and, ultimately, conflates the two, such that 'making good' (doing justice) comes to be equated with 'making safe' (doing security). While there is nothing wrong with the integration of security and justice – indeed we argue for a similar integration later – the result may be a system which is increasingly effective in achieving security, by virtue of its focus on risk-minimisation, but less effective in achieving a sense that justice has been done. One question we also posed in Chapter 5 was whether the same (risk) mentality could, under different conditions, support normative programmes and substantive outcomes different from those with which that mentality is normally aligned? To put it another way, if we are to employ the risk paradigm for security purposes, what model of justice needs to be employed with it for optimal integration of the two? In what follows we suggest that such integration can best be effected through the combination of a risk-based approach that is grounded in the mobilisation of local knowledge and capacity. Contrary to those who regard risk-based practices as inherently productive of unjust effects because of their deployment of 'actuarial' techniques in the delivery of justice, we maintain that the risk mentality can be compatible with just outcomes. The extent to which the risk paradigm is compatible with just outcomes depends upon the practices and principles with which it is configured. Here, we shall argue that the integration of local capacity governance and risk-based approaches can promote outcomes that are experienced as just.

The chapter is divided into two sections. In the first section we explore the problem of inequity or 'deficit' in the governance of security and propose a model – nodal governance – for addressing it. In the second section we explore further how the model of nodal governance can be used to optimise security governance and, in so doing, can better integrate the objectives of security and justice. In order to demonstrate this we examine how the nodal model of security governance has been applied in South Africa.

## Problems and prospects in the governance of security

### Inequity and deficit in the governance of security

In earlier chapters of this book we have described how security governance has ceased to be the exclusive prerogative of the state and has come, instead, to be the collective responsibility of networks of commercial and non-commercial 'partners'. The increased application of commercial and civil solutions to issues of security governance is not, however, without its problems. In the USA, the growth of 'gated communities' has led to speculation about a future 'Fortress America' (Blakeley and Snyder, 1997). Davis's (1992) analysis of Los Angeles presages a situation in which public space is privatised, the urban landscape is militarised, video-surveillance is endemic, city life is 'feral', vigilantism is rife and those who can afford to do so retreat behind 'gated' enclaves, protected by private guards. Such developments are by no means restricted to the USA. In Sao Paulo, where recession, political corruption and high rates of murder and violence (often involving the military police) have increased tension, higher income groups take various steps to defend themselves. Some desert the city for the periphery or build secure enclaves within the centre. The wealthiest now take to the air:

> Every morning the man leaves his gated community by helicopter. He is not alone: the sky is full of helicopters taking the rich to work above an endless sprawl of high-rise blocks and streets jammed with traffic. 'Having a helicopter . . . is considered a necessary tool for existing' [said the Director of a leading helicopter manufacturer]. Sao Paulo's penchant for helicopters has grown partly as a result of its exaggerated social divides, in a country with one of the world's most unfair distributions of wealth.
>
> (Bellos, 2000)

In South Africa, a country we discuss more fully in the following section, similar difficulties prevail. Consider the following analysis contained in an article in which one of us was a co-author:

> Bluntly put, the major forms of private security that have been most active in policing the transition in South Africa have preserved, and in many ways, extended Apartheid. They have done so through catering to public demands for security that are guided by old ideas for what security 'looks like', carving up the country's landscape into an archipelago of secure 'fortified fragments' from which 'undesirables' are barred entry.
>
> (Shearing and Kempa, 2002)

South Africa has not only adopted the North American concept of the 'gated community', it has begun to take that concept to its logical conclusion: the 'gated town'. One such new development in the Western Cape uses the image of the 'safe' medieval town as a means for promoting its vision of gated security. 'Heritage Park' is surrounded by an electrified fence, its perimeter being policed by forty private guards who monitor a battery of sophisticated computer equipment. Adjacent to the complex, though out of the sight-line of its residents – and in ironic invocation of the principles of 'secured by design' – the developers have built a township of 142 modest houses on land previously set aside as a squatter camp. For the developers this is a 'win–win situation': 'They get free homes and we have dealt with an unsightly problem'. Added to that, it is hoped that residents of the settlement will provide a source of labour to Heritage Park's shops and domestic premises. The parallels with the Bantustans of the old Apartheid era should be obvious (ibid.).

It might be argued that the inequities arising from Heritage Park are atypical: that the application of neo-liberal principles during rapid, post-Apartheid transition engenders a pathology specific to South Africa. Yet, it is also apparent that changes to security governance arising under neo-liberalism pose general problems for all societies. Consider two of the developments described in this book: the growing plurality of agents involved in security governance and the increased preoccupation of those agents with risk-based thought and action. These developments raise two problems. On the one hand, diversity in the provision of security might give rise to a fragmented system which combines the worst of all worlds: ineffectiveness, due to lack of co-ordination between the elements; and injustice, due to inequity in the distribution of services. On the other hand, preoccupation with risk – and particularly with the view that every risk justifies a security response – might lead to the emergence of overly invasive form of security (Johnston, 2000a).

Some of these problems are already evident in North America and Europe. In Britain two centuries ago those who could afford private protection objected to contributing taxes towards the establishment of the 'new police'. Nowadays, prosperous taxpayers in North America also complain about having to 'pay twice' for security: once to the government and once to the commercial companies they employ to protect them. Of course, this demand for tax reform threatens to exacerbate the unequal distribution of risk, since those who are most interested in reducing taxes are also those who are most likely to enjoy the highest levels of objective security – not least because they spend so much of their time in privately protected places (Bayley and Shearing, 1996). A further complication is added by the differential quantity and quality of public security delivered to rich and poor communities. In particular, the increased application of paramilitary police techniques in areas of urban deprivation (Davis, 1992; Kraska and Kappeler, 1997) means that poor people tend to receive the maximum quantity of police 'force' and the minimum quality of police 'service': or, to put it another way, the poor get justice and the rich get security. This situation is dangerous in two respects. First, there is the prospect that those with the loudest voices and the largest pockets will demand access to the best services in order that their insecurities are met. With the consequent inequity that that implies comes the danger that security becomes polarised, the rich having access to both commercial and public police services, the poor being left to enjoy the dubious benefits of a residual public police force; a future which Bayley has referred to as 'a poor police policing the poor' (Bayley, 1994: 144). Second, as the commercial sector makes greater and greater inroads into policing, concern will grow that unregulated market forces are incompatible with the effective co-ordination of public security that partnership, itself, demands.

One way of dealing with inequity is to enable poor people to participate in markets for security (Shearing, 1995; Bayley and Shearing, 1996). For this to happen a means has to be found to re-allocate public funding towards security. One way of doing this is to provide block grants to communities, enabling them to purchase various mixtures of public and private policing. This approach could have a number of benefits: it could help to iron out inequities; it could lead to the development of security regimes appropriate to the needs of particular communities; and it could invest direct authority in the hands of those most affected by existing inequities. In addition to that, such reforms would affirm the indivisibility of security: the fact that whereas the well-to-do already pay for crime, they 'have not learned that they will save more by levelling up security than by ghettoising it' (Bayley and Shearing, 1996: 603).

This type of approach is consistent with the objectives of 'optimal' security. An optimal system of security may be defined as one which is neither quantitatively excessive (to the detriment of objectives other than security) nor qualitatively invasive (to the detriment of personal freedoms) and which satisfies conditions of collective accountability, effectiveness and justice (compare Johnston, 2000a: 180). One of the objectives of the optimal model would be to develop security as a collective good (Loader and Walker, 2001). In the past, of course, the state (the 'public sphere') has been regarded as the essential repository of the collective good. Yet, for reasons we have outlined previously it is no longer possible to conceive the state in this way. Nowadays, the state is but one player – albeit an important one – in a complex network of governing agencies. The challenge for democratic government is to ensure that the actions of the various commercial and civil bodies which participate in government accord, as much as possible, with the collective good. To argue this is not to deny the real tensions and conflicts that divide governing agents, it is merely to insist that there are no immutable contradictions between the objectives of commercial, civil and collective partners. Thus, in the case of commercial security it is necessary to consider how, in a market economy, governmental mechanisms can be put into place that ensure the collective good is protected in security networks composed, in part, of commercial elements. One way of approaching these issues is through the concept of nodal governance.

## *Nodal governance*

The governance of security is increasingly complex. On the one hand, states continue to have a major role in security governance, the state sector of criminal justice being more extensive than ever. On the other hand, a growing pluralisation of security governance is evident, estimates suggesting that commercial police outnumber public police by a ratio of almost two to one in Britain (Johnston, 2000a), two to one in India (Kempa *et al.*, 1999), between two and three to one in North America (Swol, 1998; Rigakos and Greener, 2000), five to one in Hong Kong (Johnston, 2001a), and between five and seven to one in South Africa (Irish, 1999; Schoenteich, 2000). This pluralisation or 'multi-lateralisation' (Bayley and Shearing, 2001) of security governance has been explained, primarily, in terms of the state's 'devolution' or 'dispersal' of certain policing functions to the non-state sector under neo-liberal conditions. Thus, it has been claimed that an increasingly 'hollowed-out' state (Rhodes, 1994) has employed privatisation policies to disburse some 'peripheral' security functions to the commercial sector, leaving 'core' functions in the hands of state police (Cope *et al.*, 1995). While it is certainly true that the state has played a key role in its own 'self-deconstruction', exercising strategies of 'rule at a distance' in order better to demarcate core ('steering') functions from peripheral ('rowing') ones (Osborne and Gaebler, 1993), what has occurred is far more complex than the mere devolution of state functions under the pressures of neo-liberalism. For concurrent with the devolution of state functions to non-state auspices, there has also been an emergence of new forms of governance outside state parameters (Elkins, 1995; Shearing and Wood, 2000; Braithwaite, forthcoming). Consider an example. While the emergence of risk-based policing has been linked primarily to the rise of neo-liberalism (O'Malley and Palmer, 1996), we demonstrated in Chapter 5 that its emergence reflects what the corporate sector has being doing for decades to promote security. Thus, while talk of 'devolution' or 'dispersal' from state to non-state agencies has provided useful analytical insights into the changing character of policing, it has also obscured the extent to which many developments have taken place through the activities of 'private governments' (Mcauley, 1986) without recourse to the state.

In a recent analysis (Hermer *et al.*, 2002) it has been argued that while state policies of privatisation and dispersal have been partly responsible for pluralising the governance of security, state-based legal frameworks – founded on the 'public'/'private' distinction – have played a major enabling role. Thus, state property law has provided the framework within which corporations act as 'private' property owners in assuming a role in the governance of security. One implication of this analysis is that we need to take account of the linkages and relationships that connect state and non-state nodes of governance and which underpin their activities. Yet, state-led conceptions of governance have been unable to recognise the relational quality of contemporary governance. For example, the 'steering' and 'rowing' analogy, while providing useful descriptive insights into governmental strategies, is predicated on a non-relational view of governance: one which sees governance as the mere power of one agent *over* another, rather than as a varying relationship *between* agents. Accordingly, the state-led approach has been unable to theorise what one of us has called the 'new morphology of governance': 'the increasingly amorphous space occupied *inter alia* by formal political institutions, non-governmental organisations, commercial entities, "private governments", voluntary agencies and civil bodies' (Johnston, 2000a: 162). Indeed, even those approaches that have eschewed state-led conceptions of governance while retaining, albeit grudgingly, some of their conceptual machinery, have fared little better. The view that state sovereignty is undermined by the increasingly 'blurred boundaries' of the 'public–private divide' – a view previously articulated by each of the present authors – fares little better. For, as one of us has recently expressed it: 'It is not merely that the boundaries between state and non-state institutions have developed "blurred edges", those boundaries have been transformed, sometimes coagulating into specific configurations, sometimes dissolving back into themselves or into one another' (ibid.: 162).

In order to understand the linkages and relationships that connect state and non-state nodes of governance it is necessary to dispense with the 'boundary'-based model of governance – itself the product of an increasingly tenuous model of 'territorially'-based state sovereignty (see Elkins, 1995) – and invoke, instead, a network-based approach. In short, it is necessary to adopt a nodal, rather than a state-centred, conception of governance (see also Shearing and Wood, 2000; Kempa *et al.*, 1999). Within this conception of governance no set of nodes is given conceptual priority. Instead, the exact nature of governance, and the precise contribution of the various nodes to it, are matters for empirical enquiry. For that reason the specific ways in which governmental nodes relate to one another will vary across time and space. Undoubtedly, of course, the governmental arrangements that exist in certain places may become entrenched for considerable periods of time, but particular governmental configurations should be seen as the product of specific empirical conditions rather than as the expression of essential characteristics. Today, we are witnessing a period in which the empirical regularities we once took for granted are changing rapidly. More than that, the relationship between different nodes of governance is by no means uniform, the agents involved being in various states of co-operation and conflict. In Britain, for instance, there has been mutual hostility and suspicion between the commercial and state security sectors over matters of scope and influence. Yet, there has also been both commercial sponsorship of state policing (Johnston, 1992b) and state sponsorship of commercial security (Johnston and Donaldson, forthcoming), confirmation of the fact that resources may flow across nodes in a variety of different ways (Grabosky, forthcoming).

There is much work to be done in mapping this changing morphology of governance and it is interesting to speculate on how the task of nodal cartography might develop. At present, a distinction may be drawn between four significant sets of governmental nodes: the state sector, the corporate or business sector, the sector composed of non-governmental organisations and the informal or voluntary sector. However, our nodal cartographer is less interested in the structural alignment of nodes than in analysing the relationships between them. Consider two issues. First, obvious questions will arise about the legal conditions which underpin different nodal-relational patterns: questions, for example, about the enabling and disenabling features of state and international laws and consistency and inconsistency within and between them. Second, there will be questions about the relational capacities of different nodes. For example, much debate has focused on the state's capacity to regulate the commercial security sector, and in many jurisdictions the 'solution' to the 'problem' of security governance is assumed to be the state's effective regulation of commercial companies. However, the general problematic of state regulation fails to capture the complexity of nodal regulatory practices. For while states undoubtedly continue to engage in regulatory activity, it is increasingly apparent that much of the regulation that occurs is carried out under non-state auspices (Scott, 2002). Thus, within nation states, professional bodies, trade associations and insurance companies undertake regulatory activities while, at the global level, equivalent activities are carried out by non-state bodies such as the International Monetary Fund and the World Bank. Accordingly, one critical emphasis of the nodal model is that states are both the subjects and objects of regulation (Braithwaite, 2000) and relate to each other within a complex terrain of 'regulatory space' (Shearing, 1993).

The nodal approach has several important implications. First, it stresses that only by refusing to give conceptual priority to the state does it become possible to consider the range of governmental nodes that exist and the relationships between them. Second, by emphasising that the state is no longer a stable locus of government, the model defines governance as the property of networks rather than as the product of any single centre of action. Third, as a relational model, this approach defines governance as the property of shifting alliances rather than as the product of (state-led) 'steering' and 'rowing' strategies. Fourth, the approach affirms the obvious, but frequently ignored fact that every form of governance is a product of human invention and re-invention and, as such, has normative implications.

## Optimising security through nodal governance

### Local capacity building

Pursuing this last point the nodal model enables us to think afresh about how to re-configure security governance in the 'optimal' direction referred to previously. In particular, by linking up – or 'networking' – non-state nodes of security with each other, and with state nodes, it is possible that some of the strengths of 'private' forms of provision may be maximised, and some of their dangers minimised. This is, of course, no easy task. While we wish to emphasise the importance of local planning and capacity building in the construction of democratic forms of security governance, we would admit that, so far, most forms of 'local capacity governance' – notably those associated with the emergence of mass private property and the growth of gated communities – have favoured the wealthy rather than the poor and, by so doing, have given nodal governance a distinctly 'feudal' resonance. Having said that, there is no inherent reason why local capacity building should be restricted to the wealthy or to the domain of private governments. Wood's (2000) recent research has shown how during the 1990s in Ontario, Canada, local governments, under the neo-liberal banner of 'The Common Sense Revolution' took a lead from their private counterparts and began to view security as a commodity. As well as initiating new forms of accountability that emphasised fiscal prudence and customised service delivery, municipal governments also began to prioritise local definitions of security. Far from relying exclusively or primarily on public police for their accomplishment, however, these local definitions assumed that security would be the prerogative of a network of service providers rather than of any single agency. This led, in turn, to the Ontario Provincial Police setting itself the goal of becoming 'the service provider of choice' to its municipal clients. In effect a situation developed where explicit recognition was given to the role of networked governance in the construction and pursuit of local security priorities.

The Patten Commission on policing in Northern Ireland (Independent Commission, 1999; Shearing, 2001; Shearing and Kempa, 2002) whose membership included one of the authors provided a sustained attempt to apply some of the principles of nodal governance to the democratisation of security. The Commission started out from three propositions: that policing must work towards the protection of human rights; that it must mobilise local knowledge and capacity in both the direction and delivery of policing; and that policing practice must be responsive to local objectives and concerns as well as transparent and democratically accountable. Central to the Commission's approach was the recommendation that the state establish a 'Policing' (rather than a 'Police') Budget to be administered by a 'Policing' (rather than a 'Police') Board. In proposing the establishment of a Policing Board, the Commission's aim was to set up an administrative body responsible for putting together and regulating networked arrangements for security governance that would be both democratic and effective. The Board's role in this regard would consist of three components. First, it would develop plans through extensive discussion with agents interested in promoting security including the police, private security and community organisations. Second, it would facilitate the implementation and maintenance of such programmes by acting as the body responsible for controlling the flow of funds into the security network. Third, it would act as a monitoring body holding all nodes within the network accountable for their decisions and actions.

In order to facilitate this, the Commission recommended that the Policing Board should have full legal powers to scrutinise the actions of all policing bodies after the fact. By so doing, it replaced the principle of 'operational independence' (the usual legal foundation for affirming the primacy of state policing) with the notion of 'operational responsibility' (an alternative legal basis for navigating the plurality of networked security governance). By placing control of the state budget for policing in the hands of a public agency other than the police, and by allowing that agency to fund and scrutinise the activity of plural security nodes, the Commission hoped that the state could extend its involvement in public security beyond conventional (police) boundaries and, by so doing, facilitate the development of locally generated security projects (note the relationship between this method of funding and the objectives of block grants discussed earlier). Any unacceptable practices or outcomes arising from such local initiatives could be dealt with either through legal sanction or through termination of funding. The Commission also proposed the creation of 'District Policing Partnership Boards'. These Boards would be responsible for the development of networked security at the district level and for ensuring that participants within the emerging networks worked together harmoniously in order to achieve effective and legitimate policing. Such Partnership Boards would be permitted to raise taxes at the local level in order to support the development of equitable nodal policing arrangements at district level. Inappropriate conduct by participating partners would, again, be dealt with by the withdrawal of funding or through alternative municipal mechanisms such as the denial of licensing applications.

The proposals contained in the Patten Commission Report give an indication of how the nodal model might be applied to the problem of re-configuring security governance. It is important to emphasise that the notion of Policing Budgets, is intended not just to allow poor people to buy security. It is also intended to re-direct tax resources in the furtherance of democracy, empowerment, justice and security. The relationship between the last two of these – security and justice – has, of course, been a central issue in this book.

In the following section we explore the relationship between security and justice further by once again applying the nodal model, this time to security governance in South Africa. Our contention here is that the South African model provides one example of how the mentalities of risk and justice can be conjoined in order better to reconcile the demands of security and justice. We will subsequently consider other possibilities for doing this that relate to the integration of risk and restorative justice. The model also provides an example of how within a context of a nodal framework the governance of security can become integrated with other governmental objectives and concerns.

## The Zwelethemba Model

Finding ways of reconciling security and justice has been a central plank of work undertaken in South Africa by a project team under the direction of one of the authors. The model was first developed in conjunction with people living in Zwelethemba, a poor black informally-housed community near Cape Town, whose name means 'place of hope'. A project team began working in Zwelethemba in 1998 and remained there for two years. The aim of the scheme was to build a model of 'local capacity policing' that would both recognise and utilise the ability and knowledge of the men and women who lived in the community. In order to do this the project aimed to enhance both community security and justice while, all the time, remaining committed to the furtherance of local democracy and the protection of participants' human rights. An inquiry undertaken at the beginning of the project had revealed widespread support for community-based schemes for governing security (to tackle the routine security problems and fears which marred people's everyday lives ) that people would consider just. The pilot project aimed to develop the mentalities, institutions, technologies and practices through which communities could facilitate the resolution of local disputes (peacemaking) and respond to generic issues that were contributing to insecurity (peacebuilding). The focus on disputes recognised that disputes (broadly conceived) were the source of much of the insecurity within Zwelethemba. The focus on peacebuilding recognised that disputes very often arose out of recurrent generic problems within communities.

The principal institutional means for achieving these aims is through the formation of Peace Committees that receive reports of disputes and convene Gatherings to resolve them. The first step in this process is to interview the disputants in order to identify individuals in the community who are thought to have the knowledge and capacity to help resolve the dispute. The disputants are then asked whether they would be willing to attend a Gathering to which the persons identified will be invited. At the Gathering the members of the Peace Committee attending (a minimum of two) will facilitate a process whereby those invited to help in the resolution are encouraged to outline a plan of action to establish peace. Peace, in this context, involves promoting a state of affairs that will, it is thought by the Gathering's participants, reduce the likelihood that the dispute will recur/continue. A key skill of Peace Committee members is to shift the focus away from what happened in the past to what can be done in the future.

While this future or risk-focus is consistent with much that has been taking place within corporate realms in the governing of security, it was not something that was directly imported from these realms. Rather it emerged in the course of the 'experimentation' that took place in the course of the pilot project. A future focus it was found fitted with the widespread desire of participants at Gatherings to leave the past behind in order to get on with the business of living together in the future. A critical condition shaping this desire was that there were few exit possibilities from peoples' living situations – people were stuck with each other for the foreseeable future. Within this context dealing with the past proved less compelling than creating a 'better tomorrow'.

A second crucial feature of the process developed during the pilot project was an insistence that it was not for Peace Committee members who were the problem solvers but for the participants in the Gatherings. The role of Peace Committee members was to facilitate a process in which participants would be able to fully mobilise their knowledges and capacities. Peace Committee members are neither adjudicators nor problem-solvers but facilitators in the initiation of peace.

Gatherings are concluded when a resolution is agreed upon and those present commit themselves to a plan of action. If the problem cannot be resolved, and if one of the parties to the dispute wishes to take the problem to the police, Peace Committee members will help them to do so. Local police are aware of, and endorse, the work of Peace Committees. Indeed the programme was initiated with the support of the national police and the Ministry of Justice.

A final critical feature of the Zwelethemba Model is that at no time is force used or threatened.

Several points are worthy of note about the process of peace-making now that a robust model has emerged that is being 'rolled out' to other communities. First, in the initial stages, external coaches (typically from neighbouring communities) help Committee members to develop their facilitative skills. Soon, however, internal coaches are identified from within the Committee so as to ensure that learning is both localised and continuous. Second, an essential part of the model involves the collection of data. This takes place as part of a review process in which audit teams both analyse the range of problems arising and also monitor what happens in every Gathering. As well as analysing the reports of Gatherings, the audit team carries out interviews with a random sample of those attending in order to generate an independent source of information about the validity of the reports they receive. In addition to data gathering and analysis, surveys are carried out in order to assess the nature of community problems and the steps which people take to resolve them. By these various means transparency is ensured and feedback given to Peace Committees and to their coaches.

A third point is worth re-iterating. Like family group conferencing, the aim of peacemaking is to bring together local knowledge and capacity in order to produce a solution. However, the aim of this process is the purely instrumental one of problem solving. While peacemaking has links to restorative justice, it does not aspire to restorative outcomes, such as using restoration as healing for victims, as a means by which offenders might accept responsibility for their actions, or as a mechanism by which communities might denounce wrongful behaviour. While frequently symbolic acts, such as holding hands, take place they operate to confirm a commitment to future courses of action.

Finally, while the model remains neutral about what constitutes 'resolution' of a problem, it is firmly grounded in the principle of shifting attention from the past to the future. As we have already suggested there are a number of reasons for this future-oriented focus. For one thing, communities typically emphasise that the disputes put before Peace Committees are not merely 'past' events in need of retrospective resolution, but are also ongoing interpersonal and community concerns. A dispute about a noisy neighbour is not merely 'owned' by the offender and the victim but is also the property of a wider community having a stake in the future management of the problem. For another thing, the model has a distinct family resemblance with the corporate mentality of governance described in Chapter 5. There we argued that the mentality which infuses corporate governance is quite different from that found in a criminal justice system dominated by the punishment paradigm. Since corporate security managers are unconcerned with rectifying past wrongs, they refuse to accord punishment any special status as a governing technique. Instead, their sole concern is with managing risks in order, better, to govern the future. Clearly, this corporate approach suggests a model of justice which is quite different from that found in the criminal justice system, not least because it is predicated upon a new conception of the relationship between justice and security. We return to this point in a moment.

The second pillar of the work of Peace Committees is peace building or community building. This involves actions taken to respond to the generic problems identified in peacemaking Gatherings and in surveys . Of these generic factors the most damaging and persistent ones are poverty and the lack of legitimate opportunities existing for gainful employment, issues that cut across almost every problem identified and every Gathering convened. Another is the lack of infrastructure within communities as witnessed, for example, in the absence of adequate facilities for children.

While generating many good ideas about how to address these generic problems (often through Committee-initiated Gatherings to consider generic issues), Peace Committees during the pilot phase were constantly faced by the absence of necessary resources for implementing them. In view of this, a key aim identified during the pilot phase was to find a mechanism that would make resources available to Peace Committees in a way that enabled them to undertake peace-building initiatives and also to sustain their own work.

The issue of sustainability proved to be both a crucial and a difficult one. Participants in peacemaking forums, during the pilot phase, often raised the 'free rider' problem saying, 'we do all of this work from which the community benefits; but we get no compensation and the members of our households would prefer us to spend the time earning some money instead'. However, the project team, and community members involved in the Zwelethemba 'experiment' were very aware that the 'obvious' solution to the problem – paying participants for their work – would merely replicate the failures of previous reform programmes undertaken by governmental and non-governmental organisations in South Africa. It was clear, for example, that turning the work into paid employment simply gives rise to another layer of 'experts', divorced from the community, and creates divisive status distinctions between the different groups. The model that has developed seeks to get around this problem by recognising both the material value of the Committees' work to its members and to the community, and the administrative costs associated with carrying it out. To achieve these aims a payment structure has been built into the model. Committees earn a monetary payment for every 'successful' Gathering held. (The money for this has to date been raised both through donor funding and through local councils though, in the longer term, it is anticipated that this money, together with that required to support the wider programme, will come from governments rather than from donors.) 'Success', in this instance, does not presuppose a resolution of a dispute: merely that the processing of a particular case has conformed with the principles and procedures – a Code of Good Practice and Steps – to which Committee members have subscribed. The money obtained is ploughed back into local development projects, linked to the generic problems identified. Thus, for each monetary payment (at the time of writing R200 or approximately US$20), 10 per cent supports the administrative expenses of the Peace Committees; 60 per cent goes into a community fund for peace-building projects; the final 30 per cent goes 'into the pockets' of the Committee members who were involved in facilitating the Gathering to recognise the value of the work they do. This contrasts sharply with most programmes that seek to mobilise the fourth, civil society, sector that pays for professionals but expect community members to volunteer.

Data analysed during an initial Pilot Project at Zwelethemba indicated that resolutions and commitments to courses of action took place in over 90 per cent of the Gatherings and that the delay between report and resolution was usually no more than a few days. Two other findings were significant. First, women and young people played a major role in Gatherings both as Committee members and as peacemakers. Second, it was demonstrated that Peace Committees dealt effectively with serious problems such as domestic violence that might not come to the attention of the police or might only be dealt with by police reluctantly. In an extension of the programme to other communities in the Western Cape and other provinces local Organisers (who work with one or two Peace Committees) and Co-ordinators (who have a wider mandate) have been employed to take on the job of recruiting Peace Committees and, once having done so, to facilitate and monitor their work. Organisers and Co-ordinators are either recruited from the Committees themselves or are part of local networks, sympathetic to the schemes objectives, such as women's networks and networks of co-operatives. Organisers and Co-ordinators, like the Committees they support, are paid on an outcome basis and their work is also subject to audit. This focus on outputs is important since the model aims to ensure that the peacemaking and peace-building processes can be funded in a way that conforms with the effective use of tax resources. The model is predicated on a 'no product, no support' mentality.

In summarising the main features of the Zwelethemba model four points should be emphasised. First and foremost, the model draws upon the idea that the provision of block grants for poor people, funded from the tax system, can be used to address the problems of inequality and inequity in the distribution of security (Shearing, 1995; Bayley and Shearing, 1996) and can also offer a basis for developing new forms of security governance (Independent Commission, 1999). Second, the model implicitly raises the question: 'what is good and bad about risk-based modes of security governance that have come to characterise the corporate governance of security?' An obvious implication behind this question is that corporate security governance is double-edged. On the one hand, the massive expansion of private security that has occurred in North America and, latterly, in South Africa has exacerbated already existing structural inequalities between rich and poor. While the rich retreat behind security gates, watched over by armed guards and CCTV cameras, the poor are left to rely on their own devices or on the services of an increasingly stretched public police apparatus. From this aspect corporate governance threatens to increase existing divisions and tensions within and between communities and to add to the general 'governance deficit' which exists between rich and poor people throughout the world. On the other hand, it is clear that corporate modes of security governance empower significantly those consumers who have the material means to participate in them. As a result, groups of consumers, such as those living in gated communities, are able to exercise choice over the quantity and quality of security they experience and, by so doing, declare themselves relatively autonomous with respect to state security auspices. This dual character of corporate governance provides a normative agenda that the Zwelethemba helps us to address. Its aim was to develop a model for the nodal governance of security that would enhance the autonomy of local communities but would do so without generating the pathological consequences associated with corporate developments.

Third, there is the question of the relationship between the

Zwelethemba model and state governance. Here, again, a duality has to be considered. On the one hand, the model promotes the local governance of security through forms of self-direction which are compliant with state law and which make no attempt to challenge the state's claim to monopolise the distribution of physical force. On the other hand, the model should, in no way, be seen as equivalent to a state-led strategy of 'responsibilisation' in which people are mobilised to act in accordance with state objectives, and where the community merely provides human and other resources for the delivery of state agendas. To put it another way, the Zwelethemba model does not subscribe to a neo-liberal strategy of security governance whereby the state 'steers' and the community 'rows'. On the contrary, the model is based on a process in which governments provide support to local people who, themselves constitute a significant node in the governance of security.

Having reviewed the model we turn now to a central question of this chapter and this book, namely, how it might be possible to do both security and justice without recourse to the thinking and practices that lie at the heart of the punishment model or more generally a retributive model? Specifically, is it possible to think of, and more importantly to experience, justice within a context that is not past-oriented and that does not require the balancing of past wrongs with the authoritative imposition of a present burden or, even more, a present pain? Put in yet another way, is it possible to conjoin security and justice within a framework that is future-focussed? Or again, can we imagine, and then realise in practice, a model for integrating security and justice that is as simple and parsimonious as the one embedded in the punishment paradigm but that produces very different consequences?

The Zwelethemba model was developed, and is being 'rolled out', within a context in which both the informal institutions developed for doing justice (street committees) and the formal ones (the criminal justice system) view authoritative adjudication by an independent impartial agent and the meting out of sentences that impose a burden (typically involving pain/suffering) as the only acceptable way of accomplishing justice and promoting security. What is striking about the work of Peace Committees is that they offer a very different way of accomplishing security (a safer tomorrow) through a process that participants (both disputants and others) consider to be just without the resort to either punishment or even the imposition of a burden through the judgement of an authoritative agent. How is this accomplished?

We would argue that three features of the process are critical. First, the opportunity to pursue security and justice through the formal criminal justice system remains open both because there is no requirement to report a dispute to a Peace Committee and because it is always possible to take the matter to the police once such a report has been made. (As the agreements entered into in a Gathering are never imposed and there is no requirement to admit guilt the issue of double jeopardy does not arise.) Second, Gatherings are not premised on a bifurcation of the disputants into victims and offenders. Disputes are understood as ongoing processes (not past and sealed) in which the roles of victim and offender oscillate. In a dispute one party might be a 'victim' today, might have been an 'offender' yesterday and may become an 'offender' again tomorrow. This mitigates against those approaches which try to make up moral wrongs and to do justice according to an essentialist opposition between victims and offenders.

Third, not only are the material elements of the dispute typically addressed (return of goods, payment of medical expenses and so on) but moral 'losses' where they exist (such as having the right not to have ones property disrespected) are also addressed. However, these matters are not addressed through a backward looking process that seeks to balance wrongs with burdens but through a forward looking one that seeks to guarantee that the disputants moral goods will be respected in the future. Contrary to what one might expect from the discourses of many moral philosophers with a deontological approach, this is experienced as both a just and an instrumentally effective outcome. Justice, as a moral outcome, is given meaning within a future-focused framework.

This last issue is particularly important. What we are suggesting is that the Zwelethemba model seems to provide a forward looking framework for doing justice that people are intuitively comfortable with. Resolutions are considered just not merely because harms are dealt with but because they are dealt with in a way that generates a sense that justice has been done equivalent to the subjective experience of justice provided to people within a retributive process. It is necessary, therefore, to consider the moral reasoning that lies behind people's engagement with a system of justice that, while intuitively compelling, does not rely on a backward looking retributive model. In a recent paper, McDermott (2001) argues that wrongdoers incur two debts to the victim: a material debt that has to do with the material harm done; and a moral debt that has to do with the moral wrong done. While restitution, he suggests, can respond effectively to the material debt it cannot respond to the moral debt since the nature of the two debts incurred is qualitatively different. To put it another way: material goods are transferable; moral goods are not. In view of this, McDermott argues that punishment is a permissible treatment because it deprives wrong-doers of moral goods, namely, the right to be treated in a particular way, in much the same fashion that the wrongful act deprived the victim of the right be treated in a particular way.

How does this analysis relate to what occurs in Zwelethemba? Here people feel that justice is done when past moral wrongs are dealt with by a treatment that reduces the likelihood of such wrongs re-occurring. In other words, they feel intuitively comfortable that an outcome is just and that a moral wrong has been righted when some guarantee is given that the circumstances precipitating the complaint will not re-occur thereby ensuring that their rights will be respected. While the offer of a guarantee might involve the partici-pation of the wrongdoer, such participation is neither necessary for the process nor required by the participants. What *is* necessary, however, is that people believe they will be protected from future wrong doing. Contrary to what McDermott's analysis claims, then, a transfer of moral goods appears to occur in the Zwelethemba model. 'Victims' are in receipt of a moral good – that their rights will be respected – which, hitherto, they did not possess. In that regard people in Zwelethemba, like the corporate actors described in Chapter 5, share the view that just outcomes can arise from the transfer of forward-looking (moral) guarantees. One thing which facilitates this process was mentioned earlier: the fact that both communities reject the essentialised dyad of wrongdoer and victim. In Zwelethemba actors see people as moving back and forth between the roles of offender and victim and it, therefore, makes no sense to essentialise one or the other. What does make sense is to find the means to end acts of wrongdoing by future-oriented means.

In summary, drawing upon the nodal principle, the model attempts to re-configure security and justice in two different ways. First, security and justice are conjoined by the model's future-oriented focus. Thus, justice occurs when the effects of a dispute are ameliorated *and* when the likelihood of its continuation or recurrence are reduced. In other words, the acts of 'doing justice' and 'doing security', far from being separate and distinct – even less, in tension with one another – are mutually interdependent, each one ceasing to have meaning without the other. Second, the model not only denies that security and justice are contained within the exclusive domain of the state criminal justice system, it also re-locates the two within the wider sphere of economic and political development and by so doing confirms their mutuality. Thus, the disbursement of funds ensures that by 'doing justice', Peace Committees are also making a tangible financial contribution to the process of 'doing security'.

## Conclusion

The Zwelethemba model offers an example of how the nodal approach can help us to re-think relations between security and justice and, by so doing, re-configure their governance. We are not, of course, claiming that the South African model is an 'off-the-peg' solution that will apply in all places at all times. Neither are we suggesting that local capacity building is a panacea for the problems of security governance. After all, participatory government has had a chequered history, sometimes producing limited change, sometimes being hijacked for repressive ends. However, the main strength of the nodal model is that it enables us – indeed requires us – to situate debates about security governance within a strategic and normative framework. There are two reasons for this. First, the model refuses to prioritise any particular locus of power, seeing governance as a relationship contained within a shifting network of alliances rather than as a product of the realisation of governing 'interests'. Second, the model refuses to posit any correspondence between mentalities, the objectives, institutions and technologies associated with them, and governmental 'outcomes'. For that reason we have been able to ask in this chapter whether the same mentality might, under different conditions, support normative programmes and substantive outcomes different from those with which it is normally associated. To place emphasis on the strategic and normative aspects of governance is not, of course, to ignore the existence of power inequalities within nodal networks. Neither does the nodal model deny the state's role as an important locus of governance. Our point is merely that with demonstrable evidence of nodal governance becoming more and more apparent, opportunities may arise to transform networked relations in ways that could, under the right conditions, advance just and democratic outcomes; and do so in a way that uses as little force as possible. Since that possibility becomes more thinkable under the nodal model than under alternative ones, we would argue that it merits both serious consideration and further development.

# BIBLIOGRAPHY

*Agitator* (2001) agitator.com/dp/

American Friends Service Committee (1971) *Struggle for Justice*, Hill & Wang.

Ascoli, D. (1979) *The Queen's Peace*, London: Hamish Hamilton.

Ashworth, A. (1997) 'Sentencing', in M. Maguire, R. Morgan and R. Reiner (eds) *The Oxford Handbook of Criminology*, Oxford: Clarendon: 1095–1135.

Bayley, D. H. (1994) *Police for the Future*, New York: Oxford University Press.

Bayley, D. H. and Shearing, C. D. (1996) 'The future of policing', *Law and Society Review*, 30, 3: 585–606.

Bayley, D. H. and Shearing, C. D. (2001) *The New Structure of Policing*, Washington, DC: The National Institute of Justice, U.S. Department of Justice.

Beccaria, C. (1764) *On Crimes and Punishments*, text online at www.crimetheory.com/Archive/Beccaria/index.html

Beck, U. (1992) *Risk Society: Towards a New Modernity*, London: Sage.

Bellos, A. (2000) 'Rich Brazilians look down on crime and traffic', *Guardian*, 7 August.

Bennett, T. (1994) 'Recent developments in community policing', in M. Stephens and S. Becker (eds) *Police Force, Police Service*, London: Macmillan: 107–29.

Bittner, E. (1991) 'The function of police in modern society', in C. D. Klockars and S. D. Mastrofski (eds) *Thinking About Police*, New York: McGraw Hill: 35–51.

Blakeley, E. J. and Snyder, M. G. (1997) *Fortress America: Gated Communities in the United States*, Washington, DC: Brookings Institution Press.

Bland, D. E. (1999) 'Risk management in insurance', *Journal of Financial Regulation and Compliance*, 7, 1: 13–16.

Bottoms, A. E. (1983) 'Neglected features of contemporary penal systems', in D. Garland and P. Young (eds) *The Power to Punish*, London: Heinemann Educational Books: 166–202.

161

Bowden, T. (1978) *Beyond the Limits of the Law*, Harmondsworth: Penguin.

Braithwaite, J. R. (1989) *Crime, Shame and Reintegration*, Cambridge: Cambridge University Press.

Braithwaite, J. R. (2000) 'The new regulatory state and the transformation of criminology', *British Journal of Criminology*, 40: 222–38.

Braithwaite, J. R. (forthcoming) 'What's wrong with the sociology of punishment' (author's draft).

Bratton, W. (1997) 'Crime is down in New York City: blame the police', in N. Dennis (ed.) *Zero Tolerance: Policing a Free Society*, London: IEA Health and Welfare Unit.

Bratton, W. (1998) *Turnaround: How America's Top Cop Reversed the Crime Epidemic*, New York: Random House.

Broder, J. F. (1984) *Risk Analysis and the Security Survey*, Boston, MA: Butterworth.

Brogden, M. and Shearing, C. D. (1993) *Policing for a New South Africa*, London: Routledge.

Bunyan, T. (1991) 'Towards an authoritarian European state', *Race and Class*, 32, 3: 19–27.

Burchell, G. (1993) 'Liberal government and techniques of the self', *Economy and Society* 22: 267–82.

Caldeira, T. P. R. (1996) 'Building up walls: the new pattern of spatial segregation in Sao Paulo', *International Social Science Journal*, 48, 1: 55–66.

Campbell, B. (1997) 'Zero homework', *Guardian*, 15 January.

Cavadino, M. and Dignan, J. (1997) *The Penal System: an Introduction*, London: Sage.

Chaudhary, V. and Walker, M. (1996) 'The petty crime war', *Guardian*, 21 November.

Clayton, T. (1967) *The Protectors: the Inside Story of Britain's Private Security Forces*, London: Oldbourne.

Cleveland County Council (1986) *Cleveland Structure Plan: People and Jobs*, Economic Development and Planning Department, Cleveland County Council.

Cohen, S. (1983) 'Social control talk: telling stories about correctional change', in D. Garland and P. Young (eds) *The Power to Punish*, London: Heinemann.

Cohen, S. (1994) 'Social control and the politics of reconstruction', in D. Nelken (ed.) *The Futures of Criminology*, London: Sage: 63–88.

COMPAS 2.0 (1999) www.northpointeinc.com/newcomp.htm

COMPAS 3.0 (2000) www.northpointeinc.com/newcomp.htm

*Computer Active* (2000) 'CCTV to look into the future', Issue 50, 13–26 January: 10.

Cope, S., Leishman, F. and Starie, P. (1995) 'Hollowing-out and hiving-off: re-inventing policing in Britain', in J. Lovenduski and J. Stanyer (eds) *Contemporary Political Studies*, Vol. 2, Belfast: Political Studies Association of the United Kingdom: 552–65.

Crawford, A. (2001) 'Joined-up but fragmented: contradiction, ambiguity and ambivalence at the heart of New Labour's Thirds Way', in R. Matthews and J. Pitts (eds) *Crime, Disorder and Community Safety*, London: Routledge: 54–80.

Critchley, T. A. (1978) *A History of the Police in England and Wales*, London: Constable.

Cunningham, W. C. and Taylor, T. (1985) *Private Security and Police in America: the Hallcrest Report I*, Boston, MA: Butterworth-Heinemann.

Davis, M. (1990) *City of Quartz: Imagining the Future in Los Angeles*, Verso: London.

Davis, M. (1992) *Beyond* Blade Runner: *Urban Control. The Ecology of Fear*, Westfield, NJ: Open Magazine Pamphlet Series.

Dean, J. (1997) 'Mallon's law', *Police Review*, 21 March: 16–18.

Dixon, D. (1999) 'Beyond zero tolerance', paper presented to *Australian Institute of Criminology, 3rd National Outlook Symposium on Crime in Australia*, 'Mapping the Boundaries of Australia's Criminal Justice System', Canberra, 22–3 March.

Donaldson, R. and Johnston, L. (2001) 'Community service', *Police Review*, 19 October: 26–7.

Douglas, M. (1992) *Risk and Blame*, London: Routledge.

Downes, D. and Morgan, R. (1997) 'Dumping the "hostages to fortune"? The politics of law and order in post-war Britain', in M. Maguire, R. Morgan and R. Reiner (eds) *The Oxford Handbook of Criminology*, Oxford: Clarendon: 87–134.

Duff, A. and Garland, D. (1994) 'Introduction: thinking about punishment', in A. Duff and D. Garland (eds) *A Reader on Punishment*, Oxford: Oxford University Press: 1–43.

Eck, J. E. and Spelman, W. (1987) 'Who ya gonna call? The police as problem busters', *Crime and Delinquency*, 33: 31–52.

Ekblom, P. (1998) *The Crime and Disorder Act. Community Safety and the Reduction and Prevention of Crime. A Conceptual Framework For Training and the Development of a Professional Discipline*, London: Home Office.

Elkins, D. J. (1995) *Beyond Sovereignty: Territory and Political Economy in the Twenty-first Century*, Toronto: University of Toronto Press.

Emsley, C. (1996) *The English Police*, Harlow: Longman.

Ericson, E. and Haggerty, K. (1997) *Policing the Risk Society*, Oxford: Clarendon.

Evans, P. B., Rueschemeyer, D. and Skocpol, T. (eds) (1985) *Bringing the State Back in*, Cambridge: Cambridge University Press.

Executive Outcomes (1998) www.eo.com/about/html

Farrington, D. P. (1997) 'Human development and criminal careers', in M.

Maguire, R. Morgan and R. Reiner (eds) *The Oxford Handbook of Criminology*, Oxford: Clarendon: 361–408.

Feeley, M. and Simon, J. (1994) 'Actuarial justice: the emerging new criminal law', in D. Nelken (ed.) *The Futures of Criminology*, London: Sage: 173–201.

Fischer, B. (1998) *Community Policing: a Study of Local Policing, Order and Control*, unpublished Ph.D. thesis, Centre of Criminology, University of Toronto.

Foucault, M. (1977) *Discipline and Punish: the Birth of the Prison*, London: Allen Lane.

Foucault, M. (1988) *Politics, Philosophy, Culture. Interviews and Other Writings 1977–84*, L. Kritzman (ed.), London: Routledge.

Foucault, M. (1991) 'Politics and the study of discourse,' in G. Burchell, C. Gordon and P. Miller (eds) *The Foucault Effect: Studies in Governmentality*, Chicago, IL: Chicago University Press.

Garland, D. (1996) 'The limits of the sovereign state: strategies of crime control in contemporary society', *British Journal of Criminology*, 36, 4: 445–71.

Garland, D. (1997) 'Of crimes and criminals: the development of criminology in Britain', in M. Maguire, R. Morgan and R. Reiner (eds) *The Oxford Handbook of Criminology*, Oxford: Clarendon: 11–56.

Garland, D. (2001) *The Culture of Control: Crime and Social Order in Contemporary Society*, Oxford: Oxford University Press.

Gelsthorpe, L. (1985) The Community Service Volunteers/Kent Initiative. Report IV. London: Community Service Volunteers.

Giddens, A. (1990) *The Consequences of Modernity*, Cambridge: Polity.

Gill, M. and Thrasher, M. (eds) (1985) 'Problems in implementing community policing', *Policy and Politics*, 13, 1: 37–52.

Gilling, D. (2000) 'Policing, crime prevention and partnerships', in F. Leishman, B. Loveday and S. Savage (eds) *Core Issues in Policing*, Harlow: Longman: 124–38.

Grabosky, P. (1999) 'Zero Tolerance policing', *Trends and Issues in Crime and Criminal Justice*, No. 102, Canberra: Australian Institute of Criminology.

Grabosky, P. (forthcoming) 'Private sponsorship of public police'.

Greene, J. R., Simon, T. M. and Levy, P. R. (1995) 'Merging public and private security for collective benefit: Philadelphia's Center City District', *American Journal of Police*, 14, 2: 3–20.

Griffiths, D. (2000) *Policing in England and Wales Between the Two World Wars*, unpublished Ph.D. thesis, University of Exeter.

Harthill, R. (2001) 'Circling paedophiles', *The Friend*, 5 January: 4–6.

Hebenton, B. and Thomas, T. (1995) *Policing Europe: Co-operation, Conflict and Control*, London: Macmillan.

Hebenton, B. and Thomas, T. (1996) 'Sexual offenders in the community: reflections on problems of law, community and risk management in the

USA and England', *International Journal of the Sociology of Law*, 24, 4: 427–43.

Hermer, J., Kempa, M., Shearing, C., Stenning, P. and Wood, J. (2002) *Policing in Canada in the Twenty-first Century*. Report to the Law Commission of Canada.

Hindess, B. (1982) 'Power, interests and the outcome of struggles', *Sociology*, 16, 4: 498–511.

Holcomb, H. J. (1999) 'Keeping tags on everything', *National Post*, 3 August.

Home Office (1995) *Review of Police Core and Ancillary Tasks*, London: Home Office.

Home Office (1998) *Joining Forces to Protect the Public*, London: Home Office.

Home Office (1999a) *Crime and Disorder Act. Guidance on Statutory Crime and Disorder Partnerships*, London: Home Office.

Home Office (1999b) *Proposals for Revising Legislative Measures on Fingerprints, Footprints and DNA Samples*, London: Home Office. (www.homeoffice.gov.uk/ppd/finger.htm)

Home Office (1999c) *Road Traffic: the Distance Over Time Speed Measuring Device Approval 1999*, London: Home Office. (www. homeoffice.gov.uk/ppd/oppu/dist99.htm)

Home Office (1999d) *Statistics on Race and the Criminal Justice System*, London: Home Office.

Home Office (2000) *News release: £70 Million for Severe Personality Disorder Assessment and Treatment Projects*, 22 September.

Home Office (2001a) *Criminal Justice: the Way Ahead*, London: Home Office.

Home Office (2001b) *The Criminal Justice and Police Act 2001: Changes to Sections 63A and 64 of Police and Criminal Evidence Act (PACE) 1984 Relating to the Retention of Fingerprints and Samples*, HOC 25/ 2001, London: Home Office.

Home Office/Department of Health (1999) *Managing Dangerous People with Severe Personality Disorders*, London: HMSO.

Hudson, B. (1996) *Understanding Justice*, Buckingham: Open University Press.

Hughes, G. (1998) *Understanding Crime Prevention: Social Control, Risk and Late Modernity*, Buckingham: Open University Press.

I'Anson, J. and Wiles, P. (1995) *The Sedgefield Community Force: the Results of a Survey of the Public's Response to the Introduction of the Force*, Centre for Criminological and Legal Research, University of Sheffield.

Ignatieff, M. (1978). *A Just Measure of Pain*, London: Macmillan.

Independent Commission on Policing for Northern Ireland (1999) *A New Beginning: Policing in Northern Ireland. The Report of the Independent Commission on Policing for Northern Ireland*.

Independent Committee of Inquiry (1996) *The Independent Committee of Inquiry into the Role and Responsibilities of the Police*, London: Police Foundation/Policy Studies Institute.

Irish, J. (1999) *Policing for Profit: the Future of South Africa's Private Security Industry*, Institute for Security Studies Monograph Series No. 39, Halfway House, South Africa: Institute for Security Studies.

Jacobson, J. and Saville, E. (1999) *Neighbourhood Warden Schemes: an Overview*, Policing and Reducing Crime Unit, Crime Reduction Research Series Paper 2, London: Home Office.

Johnston, L. (1986) *Marxism, Class Analysis and Socialist Pluralism*, London: Allen & Unwin.

Johnston, L. (1992a) 'British policing in the nineties: free market and strong state?', *International Criminal Justice Review*: 1–18.

Johnston, L. (1992b) *The Rebirth of Private Policing*, London: Routledge.

Johnston, L. (1997a) 'New Labour and the usual suspects', *The Chartist*, March–April: 14–15.

Johnston, L. (1997b) 'Policing communities of risk', in P. Francis, P. Davies and V. Jupp (eds) *Policing Futures: The Police, Law Enforcement and the Twenty-first Century*, London: Macmillan.

Johnston, L. (2000a) *Policing Britain: Risk, Security and Governance*, Harlow: Longman.

Johnston, L. (2000b) 'Transnational private policing: the impact of global commercial security', in J. Sheptycki (ed.), *Issues in Transnational Policing*, London: Routledge.

Johnston, L. (2001) *Private Policing and its Links to Public Policing*, Unit 5, Course PS301, Open University of Hong Kong.

Johnston, L. and Donaldson, R. (forthcoming) 'Community wardens and the "extended family of police"'.

Johnston, L., MacDonald, R., Mason, P., Ridley, L. and Webster, C. (2000) *Snakes and Ladders: Young People, Transitions and Social Exclusion*, Bristol: Policy Press.

Jones, J. M. (1980) *Organisational Aspects of Police Behaviour*, Aldershot: Gower.

Jones, T. and Newburn, T. (1998) *Private Security and Public Policing*, Oxford: Clarendon Press.

JSU (1999) Joint Strategy Unit at www.teesvalley-jsu.gov.uk

Kelling, G. L. and Coles, C. M. (1996) *Fixing Broken Windows*, New York: The Free Press.

Kempa, M., Carrier, R., Wood, J. and Shearing, C. (1999) 'Reflections on the evolving concept of "private policing"', *European Journal on Criminal Policy and Research*, 7, 2: 197–223.

Kemshall, H. (n.d.) 'Assessing and managing offender risk: the challenge for the probation service', *Risk and Human Behaviour: Newsletter of the ESRC Research Programme on Risk and Human Behaviour*, Issue No. 3, Swindon: ESRC.

Klockars, C. B. (1991) 'The rhetoric of community policing', in C. B. Klockars and S. D. Mastrofski (eds) *Thinking About Policing*, New York: McGraw-Hill: 530–42.

Kraska, P. B. and Kappeler, V. E. (1997) 'Militarizing American police: the rise and normalization of paramilitary units', *Social Problems*, 44, 1: 1–17.

Labour Party (1996) *Tackling Youth Crime: Reforming Youth Justice*, London: Labour Party.

Lessing, D. (1991) *Prisons We Choose to Live Inside*, Concorde, Canada: Anansi.

Lilley, R., Cullen, F. and Ball, R. A. (1989) *Criminological Theory: Context and Consequences*, Thousand Oaks, CA: Sage.

Loader, I. (1997) 'Policing and the social: questions of symbolic power', *British Journal of Sociology*, 48, 1: 1–18.

Loader, I. (2000) 'Plural policing and democratic governance', *Social and Legal Studies*, 93, 3: 323–45.

Loader, I. and Walker, N. (2001) 'Policing as a public good', *Theoretical Criminology*, 5, 1: 9–35.

Mcauley, S. (1986) 'Private government', in L. Lipson and S. Wheeler (eds) *Law and the Social Sciences*, New York: Russell Sage Foundation.

McDermott, D. (2001) 'The permissibility of punishment', *Law and Philosophy*, 20: 403–32.

McGill, B. (1999) 'Employers use tiny tools to keep eye on workers', *San Francisco Examiner*, 1 August.

McKenzie, I. (2000) 'Policing force: rules, hierarchies and consequences', in F. Leishman, B. Loveday and S. Savage (eds) *Core Issues in Policing*, 2nd edition, Harlow: Longman: 176–93.

McMullan, J. L. (1987) 'Policing the criminal underworld: state power and decentralized social control in London 1550–1700', in J. Lowman, R. J. Menzies and T. S. Palys (eds) *Transcarceration: Essays in the Sociology of Social Control*, Aldershot: Gower: 119–38.

McMullan, J. L. (1998) 'Social surveillance and the rise of the "police machine"', *Theoretical Criminology*, 2, 1: 93–117.

Mallon, R. (1997) 'Zero Tolerance – lessons from Hartlepool', paper presented to *IEA Zero-Tolerance Policing Conference*, London, 12 June.

Marx, G. (1988) *Undercover: Police Surveillance in America*, Berkeley, CA: University of California Press.

Middlesbrough Crime and Disorder Steering Group (1999) *A Strategy for Reducing Crime and Disorder in Middlesbrough 1999–2002*.

Miller, S. A. (1999) 'The eyes have it: iris recognition technology looks quite secure', *Milwaukee Journal Sentinel*, 3 August.

Mopas, M. S. and Stenning, P. C. (2000) 'Tools of the trade: the symbolic power of private security – an exploratory study', paper presented at *British Society of Criminology Conference*, Liverpool, July.

Morgan, P. (1978) *Delinquent Fantasies*, London: Maurice Temple Smith.

Morn, F. (1982) *The Eye That Never Sleeps*, Bloomington, IN: Indiana University Press.

Murray, C. (1994) *Underclass: the Crisis Deepens*, London: Institute of Economic Affairs.

Nalla, M. and Newman, G. (1990) *A Primer in Private Security*, New York: Harrow and Heston.

Nash, M. (1999a) 'Enter the "polibation officer"', *International Journal of Police Science and Management*, 1, 4: 360–8.

Nash, M. (1999b) *Police, Probation and Protecting the Public*, London: Blackstone.

Nash, M. (2000) 'Deconstructing the probation service – the Trojan Horse of public protection', *International Journal of the Sociology of Law*, 28: 201–13.

Newburn, T. ( 1998) 'Tackling youth crime and reforming youth justice: the origins and nature of New Labour policy', *Policy Studies*, 19, 3–4: 199–212.

O'Mahony, P. (1997) 'Zero tolerance policy could waste Garda time', *The Irish Times*, 11 March.

O'Malley, J. (1992) 'Risk, power and crime prevention', *Economy and Society*, 21, 3: 252–75.

O'Malley, P. (1997) 'Policing, politics and postmodernity', *Social and Legal Studies*, 6, 3: 363–81.

O'Malley, P. (1999) 'Volatile and contradictory punishment', *Theoretical Criminology*, 175–96.

O'Malley, P. and Palmer, D. (1996) 'Post-Keynesian policing', *Economy and Society*, 25, 2: 137–55.

Osborne, D. and Gaebler, T. (1993) *Re-inventing Government*, New York: Plume.

Parelli, P. (1993) *Natural Horse-man-ship*, Colorado Springs, CO: Western Horseman Inc.

Parsons, K. (1980) *Techniques of Vigilance*, Cincinatti, OH: Charles E. Tuttle.

Payne, S. (1999) 'No place to hide. Are you under surveillance?', *The Toronto Sun*, 1 August.

Pease, K. (1997) 'Crime prevention', in M. Maguire, R. Morgan and R. Reiner (eds) *The Oxford Handbook of Criminology*, Oxford: Clarendon: 963–95.

Pelletier, L. (1999) 'Wired for everything home electronics', *The Edmonton Sun*, 25 July.

Pinkerton Organization (1998) *Top Security Threats Facing Corporate America: 1998 Survey of Fortune 1000 Companies*, Chicago, IL: Pinkerton Service Corporation.

Pollard, C. (1997) 'Zero tolerance: short-term fix, long-term liability?', in

N. Dennis (ed.) *Zero Tolerance: Policing a Free Society*, London: IEA Health and Welfare Unit: 43–60.

Potter, K. (1996) 'Zero tolerance', *Police Review*, 19 July: 18–20.

Prison Reform Trust (1999) *Prison Report*, Issue 46, February.

Puentes, M. (1997) 'Public–private teaming is revitalizing downtowns', *US Today*, 18 November.

Read, S. (1997) 'Below zero', *Police Review*, 17 January: 16–17.

Reiner, R. (2000) *The Politics of the Police*, Oxford: Oxford University Press.

Reith, C. (1952) *The Blind Eye of History*, London: Faber & Faber.

Rhodes, R. (1994) 'The hollowing out of the state: the changing nature of the public services in Britain', *Political Quarterly*, 65, 2: 138–51.

Rigakos, G. and Greener, D. (2000) 'Bubbles of governance: private policing and the law in Canada', *Canadian Journal of Law and Society*, 15, 1: 145–84.

Robinson, C. D., Scaglion, R. with Olivero, J. M. (1994) *Police in Contradiction: the Evolution of the Police Function in Society*, Westport, CT: Greenwood Press.

Rose, N. (1996) 'The death of the social? re-figuring the territory of government', *Economy and Society*, 25, 3: 327–56.

Rose, N. (1999) *The Powers of Freedom*, Cambridge: Cambridge University Press.

Rose, N. (2000) 'Government and control: the institutional environment', *British Journal of Criminology*, 40, 2: 321–39.

Rose, N. and Miller, P. (1992) 'Political power beyond the state: problematics of government', *British Journal of Sociology*, 43: 173–205.

Roshier, B. (1989) *Controlling Crime: the Classical Perspective in Criminology*, Milton Keynes: Open University Press.

Rossmo, K. (1998) 'Geographic profiling', paper presented to *International Conference for Criminal Intelligence Analysts: Meeting the Challenge from Serious Criminality*, London: National Criminal Intelligence Service, 17–19 March.

Rutherford, A. (1996) *Transforming Criminal Policy*, Winchester: Waterside Press.

Sarre, R. and Prenzler, T. (2000) 'The relationship between police and private security: models and future directions', *International Journal of Comparative and Applied Criminal Justice*, 24, 1: 91–113.

Schoenteich, M. (2000) 'Fighting crime with private muscle: the private sector and crime prevention', *African Security Review*, 8, 5: available online at www.iss.co.za/Pubs/ASR/8No5/Contents.html

Scott, C. (2002) 'Private regulation of the public sector: a neglected facet of contemporary governance', *Journal of Law and Society* 29, 1: 56–76.

Shearing, C. (1993) 'A constitutive conception of regulation', in J. Braithwaite and P. Grabosky (eds) *Business Regulation and Australia's Future*, Canberra: Australian Institute of Criminology: 67–79.

Shearing, C. (1995) 'Re-inventing policing: policing as governance', in F. Sack, M. Vob, D. Frehsee, A. Funk and H. Reinke (eds) *Privatisieirung Staatlicher Kontrolle: Befunde, Konzepte, Tendenzen*, Baden-Baden: Nomos Verlagsgellschaft: 70–87.

Shearing, C. (2001) 'Punishment and the changing face of governance', *Punishment and Society*, 3, 2: 203–20.

Shearing, C. and Kempa, M. (2002) 'Microscopic and macroscopic responses to inequalities in the governance of security: respective experiments in South Africa and Northern Ireland', *Transformations*, Vol. 49, Special Issue on Transitions of Crime and Policing.

Shearing, C. D and Stenning, P. C. (1981) 'Modern private security: its growth and implications', in M. Tonry and N. Morris (eds) *Crime and Justice: an Annual Review of Research*, Vol. 3, Chicago, IL: Chicago University Press: 193–245.

Shearing, C. D. and Stenning, P. C. (1985) 'From the Panopticon to Disney World: the development of discipline', in A. N. Doob and E. L. Greenspan (eds) *Perspectives in Criminal Law*, Toronto: Canada Law Books.

Shearing, C. D. and Stenning, P. C. (1987) *Private Policing*, Thousand Oaks, CA: Sage.

Shearing, C. and Wood, J. (2000) 'Reflections on the governance of security: a normative enquiry', *Police Practice* 1, 4: 457–76.

Shearing, C. and Wood, J. (forthcoming) 'Nodal governance, democracy and the new "Denizens": challenging the Westphalian ideal', in S. Robins (ed.) *Limits to Liberation: Citizenship and Governance After Apartheid*, Heinemann.

Simon, J. (1988) 'The ideological effects of actuarial practices', *Law and Society Review*, 22: 772.

Simon, J. (1995) 'They died with their boots on: the boot camp and the limits of modern penality', *Social Justice*, 22, 1: 25–49.

Sklansky, D. (1999) 'The private police', *University of California Law Review*, 46, 4: 1165–287.

Social Exclusion Unit (2000) *Towards a National Strategy for Neighbourhood Renewal*: Report of Policy Action Team 6: Neighbourhood Wardens, London: Social Exclusion Unit.

Sparrow, A. (1999) 'Plans for vast DNA library to fight crime', *Electronic Telegraph*, Issue 1527, 31 July (www.telegraph.co.uk).

Spitzer, S. and Scull, A. (1977) 'Privatization and capitalist development: the case of the private police', *Social Problems*, 25, 1: 18–29.

Steedman, C. (1984) *Policing the Victorian Community: the Formation of English Provincial Police Forces 1856–80*, London: Routledge & Kegan Paul.

Steinberg, A. (1986) '"The spirit of litigation"; private prosecution and criminal justice in nineteenth century Philadelphia', *Journal of Social History*, 20: 231–49.

Stenning, P. (2000) 'Powers and accountability of the private police', *European Journal on Criminal Policy and Research*, 8: 325–52.

Stinchcombe, A. (1963) 'Institutions of privacy in the determination of police administrative practice', *American Journal of Sociology*, 69: 150–60.

Storch, R. (1975) 'The plague of blue locusts: police reform and popular resistance in Northern England 1840–57', *International Review of Social History*, 20: 61–90.

Storch, R. (1976) 'The policeman as domestic missionary: urban discipline and popular culture in Northern England 1850–1880', *Journal of Social History*, 9, 4: 481–509.

Swol, K. (1998) 'Private security and public policing in Canada', *Juristat*, 18, 3, Ottawa: Statistics Canada, Canadian Centre for Justice Statistics.

Taylor, I. (1999) *Crime in Context*, Cambridge: Polity.

Taylor, L., Walton, P. and Young, J. (eds) (1975) *Critical Criminology*, London: Routledge & Kegan Paul.

Texas Department of Criminal Justice (2001) www.tdcj.state.tx.us/stat/deathrow.htm

Tims, A. (2000) 'Behind bars', *Guardian: Space*, 6 April: 8–11.

Van Dijk, J. J. M. and Junger-Tas, J. (1988) 'Trends in crime prevention in the Netherlands', in T. Hope and M. Shaw (eds) *Communities and Crime Reduction*, London: Home Office Research and Planning Unit: 260–76.

Von Hirsch, A. (2000) 'The ethics of public television surveillance', in A. Von Hirsch, D. Garland and A. Wakefield (eds) *Ethical and Social Perspectives on Situational Crime Prevention*, Oxford: Hart: 59–76.

Von Hirsch, A. and Shearing, C. (2000) 'Exclusion from public space', in A. Von Hirsch, D. Garland and A. Wakefield (eds) *Ethical and Social Perspectives on Situational Crime Prevention*, Oxford: Hart.

Wilson, J. Q. and Kelling, G. L. (1982) 'Broken windows: the police and neighbourhood safety', *The Atlantic Monthly*, March: 29–38.

Wood, J. (2000) *Re-inventing Governance: a Study of Transformations in the Ontario Provincial Police*, unpublished Ph.D. thesis, University of Toronto.

Wright (2002) *Policing: an Introduction to Concepts and Practice*, Cullompton, Devon: Willan.

# INDEX